CW00970175

THE SO
OF
CARING

Batya Fulcher

To God, Who alone is wise, be the glory forever through Jesus
Christ our Lord (I Cor. 16:19b) (The Living Bible)

ACKNOWLEDGEMENTS

The Rev. Dr. Clifford Hill of C & M Ministries, Moggerhanger and Mr.David Noakes, Chairman of Hatikvah Film Trust, Steyning, Sussex for permission to include the prophetic words given to them on Mount Carmel in 1986.

The late Chris Mitchell of HM Photographic Bournemouth was the photographer commissioned to take the later photos of John and Batya.

Also I would like to thank Mrs. Pam Leggate of ASAP, Nailsea for typing the manuscript and offering invaluable advice. In addition other friends who are mentioned in the book without whom my story would be considerably impoverished. Last, but by no means least, my God-given family and the privilege of being their replacement-mother and intercessor.

CONTENTS

1. Weighed…and Found Wanting (Dan. 5:27)

"But Daddy, please don't go to work today!" I remember wailing, as I stood by the back door of our Surrey home, aged four. World War II had broken out a year earlier in 1939 and, being an only child, I felt very insecure if my father was not at home, all the more so because I never bonded with my mother. Daddy worked as an assistant Surveyor for one of the London borough councils, and was out of the home much of the time. I had forged a very close link with my father, far more through his frequent absence than presence.

I clearly recall him coming back home one evening with a pair of toy-scales, which acted as a kind of substitute when he was away! That day, in fact, I had made a bargain with him. "If you will bring me some scales," I said, "I promise I won't cry when you go out!" In retrospect, it is almost as though I needed some symbol of balance in the home! Much later, I learnt that my father was not *only* out of the home on business, but was very attracted both to the Pub and other ladies, which naturally my mother found incredibly hard and lonely. He was a heavy smoker, who had a perpetual 'smoker's cough', following his own mother's example which, in her case, proved to be due to Tuberculosis, causing her to spend a period in a sanatorium.

During the war years, bunk beds were installed in our living-room and curtained off with some very drab brown and beige material. I was put to bed early, and my mother whiled away the evening hours playing cards with a very friendly, childless couple from next door. I found it difficult to sleep, as the electric light penetrated the loosely woven curtains around my bunk bed, to say nothing of conversation and laughter, as the

1

card-game became more challenging. The French windows, like all others in the house, were draped with compulsory blackout material and, apart from the light from the moon and stars, everything out of doors at night was dark, quiet and eerie.

Those disturbed nights in my early years, and other wartime ones, when we all became used to being on the *qui vive* for air-raid warning sirens and falling bombs, established a difficult sleep-pattern in later life, and the tendency to wake at the slightest sound.

On 13th July 1942 my baby brother, Anthony Leslie, was born when I was aged six. I have to confess to feelings of gross annoyance over discovering the baby was a boy, since I had been hoping for a baby sister, for whom I had invented the name 'Patricia'. I shouted rudely at my poor mother when she presented me with the wee scrap lying in his cot, "Take him back and buy me a baby sister! I don't want *him*!" I felt cheated as my mother, for some strange reason, had tended to prepare me for a baby sister, not a brother. It took me years to come to terms with the fact that *he* was a *boy*, always would be a boy, and was not going to go away! But my shameful reaction must have been enough to give my mother post-natal depression!

I felt keenly dispossessed by my mother. Having been an only child until Tony was born, in my loneliness I longed for a sister with whom to play. My best friend from over the road was a boy, a year my senior, but Peter was *different* - he was my childhood sweetheart who let me ride his tricycle and who accompanied me to school, but a brother, ugh ….! In fact, time spent together as brother and sister was to be very infrequent for Tony and me during his babyhood.

2

Around this time, my mother was asked by a neighbour if she would agree to take in lodgers. Doubtless the extra money would have proved useful, and having others in the house would have had certain advantages during wartime. However, my mother was somewhat horrified to find out that the man came from West Africa, and was actually *black,* whereas the woman was *white!* Mixed partnerships, in those days, were neither popular nor common. To my mother's further dismay, she discovered, after letting a couple of rooms to them, that they were not honourably married!

I was absolutely petrified of this man, who often seemed to be going shopping for Black Sausage, which I thought revolting! I scarcely communicated with the woman at all, who tended to keep herself to herself in their two rooms. I used to cry with fear at first, every time this black man approached me, yet he was kindly and seemed, like most Africans, to love children. He certainly never harmed me physically in any way.

My father did not keep well and, with his continual hacking, was made exempt from fire-watching duties with the ARP (Air Raid Protection). He was in and out of hospital quite a bit during my early childhood, and eventually died a few days before my seventh birthday from Pulmonary Suppuration.

The day he died I was walking home from school, hand-in-hand with my friend, Peter, when suddenly I noticed that all the curtains were pulled everywhere in our house. This meant only one thing. "My Daddy has died!" I shared with Peter. He asked how I knew, but all I could manage to mumble was, "I just know."

This fact was confirmed as I ran into the house, and relatives and neighbours were sitting all around the front room

3

(known rather grandly as the drawing-room). A maiden great aunt, Aunty Amy, from my mother's side of the family, had come from Kent to Surrey, where we were living, with the express purpose of carting me back home with her, leaving my mother and brother to follow on a little later for the funeral, which was to take place at my aunt's local cemetery, and to which I was not be to invited. It was also planned that my mother would sell our Surrey home, and take over part of my aunt's home.

Aunty Amy shared her home with her older sister, Annie, and they were happy to allow us to use three rooms, plus kitchen and bathroom facilities. Neither of the aunts ever married, but Aunty Annie was a very motherly, bustly sort of old lady, with naturally wavy silver-grey hair. She was a superb cook and housekeeper, and really became a second mother-cum-grandmother to me, because my mother was forced to find work and put my baby brother into a nearby day-nursery. Hence, my small bother and I saw very little of each other thereafter, and my mother, whom I seldom saw, and I drifted further apart. She had always seemed remote and distracted, devoid of demonstrations of love and much more easily able to relate to her son and men-friends.

It was amazing just what Aunty Annie could rustle up for meals, using our combined wartime ration-books. It seemed that she could make a complete, nourishing meal from very little but hard, hot work. I can remember her now in a streaming galley-kitchen in winter, with the old laundry-copper boiling merrily away at one end, and the gas cooker going full blast at the other, her forehead and cheeks puce with heat! She never threw *anything* away, be it food, old clothes or whatever, always managing to turn it into something else that was tasty or useful, to say nothing of saving money. To this day, I follow Aunty Annie's thrifty example automatically, avoiding throwing out food, recycling or mending clothes, except that nowadays it is cheaper to throw away worn-out clothing and start again, whether buying new or at a charity shop.

Aunty Annie was equally skilled as a dressmaker. She had an old treadle sewing-machine, whose black wrought-iron base I had the misfortune to have to dust. Materials were not easily come by during the war, yet none of us ever lacked for clothes. I recall her making me a white floral silky party-dress for my birthday one year. She was able to cut out any garment without the aid of a pattern and would spend hours meticulously stitching to meet the clothing-needs of the whole family, disregarding her arthritic joints and her weak heart.

I could always be certain of finding Aunty Annie at home when I returned from school. Regularly there was her beaming smile and cheery Yorkshire greeting, "Hey oop, loov! Hungry are ya?" I was always ravenous by four in the afternoon, so we would go to the kitchen together, and from out of the larder would come leftovers from lunch, and crusts of bread which had been baked in the oven to make rusks, while it had been on during the morning hours.

Once I had gobbled to my heart's and stomach's content, my next task was to do the family food-shopping, armed with all the ration-books and a shopping-list. Early in life I had to learn to shop wisely and economically, and to make the very most of rationing. Aunty Annie was Commander-in-Chief of both ration-books and food purchases, and she carefully drew up a daily shopping-list with particular menus in mind for the following day.

One afternoon, I negligently broke some very precious hens' eggs, and was afraid to go home and confess! I went to our family butcher, upturned the shopping bag on to his clean pile of newspapers on his spotless, marble counter, and deposited broken eggshells and their gooey contents. He began to reprimand me but, on realising how upset I was, and how terrified of going home, he suggested I wait "'alf a mo", while he trundled into his back-room. Out he marched triumphantly bearing some duck eggs, for which he made no charge! How grateful and relieved I was for this miraculous replacement. His kindness saved the day!

In winter months, I had to light our sitting-room fire, which my mother had left ready-laid, so that the room was warm by the time she and my brother got home in the evening. Therefore, as a child, I was *forced* to have a sense of responsibility for family affairs, which made me somewhat serious and home-loving.

From the age of five, I had begun wiping the dishes for my mother, by standing on a chair next to the draining-board, and felt a great sense of achievement in being 'Mummy's little helper'. I never resented assisting, and realise how much it contributed to preparing me for life.

I attended the local primary school some fifteen minutes' walk from our home, but rarely participated in formal lessons during the war years, since we were in a target bombing area. Invariably my class-teacher and I were the only people to turn up for school during the worst of the bombing, and I often wonder if I was the cause of her pedalling nervously to school day-by-day, on her sit-up-and-beg bicycle! We spent hours in the school air-raid shelters, which were a novelty to me at first, because we never had one at home, Aunty Annie's philosophy being that the stout gate-leg dining-room table was good enough for her to shelter under, and that if her number was up, she was ready to go!

When the warning sirens went, she and I (and anyone else who happened to be around) would make a dash for the dubious cover the dining-room table afforded. It was not easy for her to bend and crawl on all fours, but she always made it in time. I like to think that it was not so much the table-top which protected us, but God's unseen hand from on High! We often sat there singing hymns at the top of our voices to drown out the noise, and our own fear, of whistling doodlebugs (flying bombs) overhead. She was a quiet, non-church-going believer in her own way, and I am sure that she prayed for protection every day. Doubtless many did during the war.

When the 'all-clear' was sounded, Aunty Annie would often say, with a smile of relief on her face, "That was a near one, loov, but it's all right now!" She would then accurately predict precisely where the enemy had scored a hit, and we never knew her to be wrong.

There was a great deal of neighbourliness during those years. We all cared deeply how others fared during a bombing-raid, and everybody knew everybody else, and invariably their affairs as well! How different it is nowadays, where one can live near to neighbours without knowing their name or even caring, so insular has society become! Most people are pathetically content with their own little house, little car, not-so-little television or plasma screen, and even 'littler', petty lives.

War makes one 'love one's neighbour as oneself', because there is a much greater sense of needing each other, belonging, caring, community.

Aunty Annie had a magnificent, illustrated family- Bible, and on special occasions this would come out of the sideboard and be looked at and read, as I leant up against her old rocking-chair. Such a strong, spiritual foundation would not be wasted *in God's economy*.

We did not seem to sing hymns in the school air-raid shelters, but I do recall that frequently we sang 'Ten Green Bottles', which was something of a contrast, and perhaps it was my favourite because of some unconscious association with my late father's addiction to booze!

Occasionally, when raids were less frequent, other people and teachers joined us in the shelter but, in essence, I missed at least two years of regular primary school teaching due to the war. It seemed good fun at the time not to be having proper lessons, but it meant that I, along with many others, failed my eleven-plus examination, which would have granted me entrance to the local, up-market, grammar school. The only girl who did pass was a friend of mine who had been evacuated to Yorkshire during the war. She was a bright little button, whose intelligence and superior knowledge were the envy of the whole class!

Aunty Amy was a schools' health visitor in Kent, but my mother's side of the family all hailed from Bradford, her father working all his life 'in t' mill'. Aunty Amy always thought herself a cut above the rest of the family, because of her nursing-training and consequent posting to the South East! She had an upper-crust English accent that was somewhere between Oxford and Bradford, and she had a habit, which drove the other family-members to distraction, of answering every comment anyone made to her with the monosyllabic, "Quite!" She made very few friends in life, and had great problems, especially in retirement, in communicating with anyone, although shyness never seemed to be the root-cause.

My mother's father had re-married when my mother was aged eleven, and my mother did not attempt to relate to her stepmother at all. Mum had gone to live with her much-loved grandmother on the death of her own mother when she was three years old, and remained there until her teens, when she and Aunty Annie moved south to live with Aunty Amy in Kent. There was no love lost between Mum and her stepmother. Grandma and Grandad seemed very unhappy together, theirs being a childless marriage.

I never took to Grandma, who lacked any defining character, but I had a great love for Grandad, who was warm, loving and a typical Yorkshireman! He always insisted on eating cheese with his fruit cake, and expected Yorkshire Pudding with almost every main meal. Were there any 'pud' left over from the first course, it would be consumed with great relish with a generous spoonful of golden syrup for 'afters'! Aunty Annie told me that, in winter months, one used to throw into the batter a handful of snow, and that *that* was the secret of a light, crisp Yorkshire Pudding!

2. Honour thy Father? (Ex. 20:12)

My maternal grandfather having re-married when my mother was aged eleven, it seemed strange that my own mother re-married when I was almost eleven, after being a widow for nearly four years. My stepfather went into the RAF in 1939, on the outbreak of war, and was a prisoner-of-war in Japan from 1942 until 1945.

He and my mother met when both had already decided to marry other people from the same family but, when my mother and future stepfather were introduced to each other by their then fiancé(e)s at a family party, they were immediately attracted to one another!

They were engaged quite quickly in the autumn of 1946 and married on Christmas Eve the same year, with snow lying on the ground. Dad was Mum's junior by six years and, prior to getting married, he had been something of a regular drinker, rather like my own father. However, with no pressure from anyone, he made up his mind that, once he was married, all drinking would cease, apart from on the very rare social occasion. I felt that this was unusual and admirable.

Dad was born in the East End of London, but had a difficult start in life and was brought up by devoted foster-parents in Kent. His adult years also had bad patches because, as a prisoner-of-war, he was most cruelly treated by the Japanese and, between 1942 and 1943, he slaved with other servicemen on the famous Burma Railway. Inevitably, such traumas put steel into his soul, and he and I often clashed.

I still missed my own father, although I had tried to push my feelings into the background, but was guilty, without realising it at the time, of going sometimes to my late father's grave to pray *to* him as well as praying to him night-by-night at bedtime, bringing a bittersweet comfort in its wake. It was many years before I realised the bondage I had brought upon myself thereby. When my mother re-married, I was myself at a tricky age and stage, and now see how I came between my mother and stepfather unintentionally, causing jealousies and arguments between Dad and me.

Within months of my mother's second marriage, Dad became very angry with me one day. He took off a very thick, wide leather trouser-belt and began lashing my back uncontrollably, while shouting blasphemous abuse. My mother pleaded with him to stop which, eventually, he did, because he was breathless. His hatred and jealousy of me had reached boiling-point, and I was very afraid. I never knew, from one day to the next, how he would behave, and I tiptoed around the house as if walking on eggshells, fearful of being myself or expressing myself freely. I did not know which was worse: his bad moods or his sweet-as-pie ones, which always very temporary. Even more disconcerting were episodes of total silence and his "I-am-not-speaking-to-you" periods which could last several weeks. Frequently he would refer to me when speaking to my mother as 'That ***** girl'. I rarely knew why I deserved such a title or what he was blaming me for, but it was a signal to steer clear of him as much as possible.

My half-sister, Susan Anne, was born prematurely, the October following my parents' December wedding. I was delighted and played an active part in her childhood-

11

development. She was the baby sister I had always wanted, and she was, in part, a reconciling factor as I made a useful, live-in nursemaid!

My parents were awarded a new council house a few weeks before Susan's birth. This was several miles away from my aunt's house, and it was a relief to leave the cramped accommodation with six of us sharing a 3-bed terraced property. However, moving does not change movers, as they take their problems with them.

The Canadian design, prefabricated two-storey house was first-class, with part central heating, so was warm and cosy. The second bedroom was cleverly divided by a partition-wall Dad made to provide Tony and me with separate rooms, thus releasing the box-room for Susan.

Even my mother began to be affected and influenced by Dad's behaviour. During an argument one day in the kitchen, she took a dinner-plate and smashed it down on my head. When it snapped in two, she looked on incredulously and with possible remorse, although whether for the broken china or me I had no idea.

Dad always revelled in showing me up in front of outsiders to demonstrate he was in charge. At my twelfth birthday-tea, to which a school-friend had been invited, I was ordered to my bedroom for some now forgotten misdemeanour and left in solitary confinement while the celebration continued. I was very embarrassed by this and apologised profusely to my classmate, who chose never to visit again, although we remained good friends at school, and I visited her.

I dreaded dirtying my white school-blouse as Dad would taunt me about it and declare loudly that my mother was not going to wear herself to a frazzle washing, drying and ironing it overnight. I was perfectly willing to do this myself when I returned home from school, but was made to feel inferior much of the time. As we were in blouses and navy knickers for post-war P.E. lessons, it was impossible not to soil the collar, especially in warm weather.

As I grew into my teenage-years, things came to such a head that I left home at seventeen and lived and worked in London. Difficulties began noticeably to arise at age fifteen, when my headmistress had particularly wanted to recommend me for acceptance by a technical school, which today would be called a college of further education. Dad had been to see her one traumatic lunchtime, after a huge disagreement, and he had threatened me, his face purple with rage, with his intention of "spifflicating" me and "swinging" for me. I had no idea what this meant, but was terrified. My headmistress was so appalled, she wrote an article for the Local Rag, but withheld names.

Dad had decided that he was not prepared to allow me to go on depending financially on him (and it must have been genuinely hard to have two step-children - Tony and me - plus his own daughter, Susan, to bring up on a very low wage, which he supplemented by working as a part-time chauffeur for my paternal uncle, yet my parents always smoked). My mother went to my aunt's house weekly to clean for them, which provided a small, extra income. There were terrible rows, with my mother often taking my side because she herself had gone to grammar school, taken matriculation, and later did in-house training as a florist until she first married at nineteen. Dad had received a very basic education and felt girls were not worth keeping at school because they would marry sooner or later.

13

Here was I, at only fifteen, without an 'O'-Level in sight, showing a special linguistic flare for French at secondary school, and wanting very much to go eventually to university to read French and become a language teacher! No amount of tearful reasoning would change Dad's mind. He told me that there were plenty of factories in the neighbourhood, and that even shelling and canning peas would enable me to earn enough for my keep, and such work required no *real* intelligence!

I was mortified, and so was my French teacher, with whom I got on especially well. Mercifully she stepped in, went to see my parents and asked us all how we would react if she took the initiative and sent me to friends of hers on the Franco-Swiss border as an *au pair*. The arrangement was for the employers to pay my return fare, so that no financial obligation would fall upon Dad whatsoever. Amazingly, Dad agreed! At least he did not have to keep me, buy new school uniform for yet another educational establishment, and my absence would put an end to *all* tension!

My French teacher was extremely kind, thoughtful and generous, and arranged personally for me to go to a photographer-contact of hers, who had a studio in his own home, in order to have my first passport-photo taken. She footed all the bills associated with obtaining travel-documentation and sent me to the airport with a gift of two pounds which, in those days, was a sizeable sum of money. But she was also loyal to my parents, visiting them in my absence and challenging any wrong attitudes in me.

I left secondary school just after my fifteenth birthday, went to my paternal grandparents' house in the Midlands for the Easter holidays, and then flew to Geneva where I was met by the husband of the couple who were to employ me as nanny to their four children, aged one-and-a-half to nine years - three boys and the eldest a girl. I had had some experience in helping bath and dress my baby sister, and had wheeled her out for walks in her pram. Susan was nearly twelve years my junior but, apart from that, I had had very little to do with children at all.

While basically it was a relief to be overseas and out of the home-situation, I felt very unready to take on such demanding, full-time working-hours. Madame was something of a slave-driver, who never gave her maid any time off, and tended to treat me similarly, for the princely equivalent of ten shillings (fifty pence) per week! The family rented most of an old village chateau, and Monsieur commuted every day across the Swiss border to work at United Nations in Geneva.

Quite contrary to my nature, Madame actually found me *lazy*, and it was some time before I genuinely realised I was supposed to work from dawn until bedtime non-stop and that, after all the children were fed, watered and in bed, I was then required to dry the supper-dishes, which the maid had washed because, very understandably, she was by then very tired. However, Madame was very kind in including me on the odd shopping jaunt to Gex, a French Alpine town, or to Geneva which I found to be a very beautiful, typically Swiss, spotless city. I saved every franc of my pocket-money to spend in Geneva, mainly buying small gifts to take back for my brother and sister.

Madame and I tolerated each other for five arduous months, by the end of which I was so bi-lingual that I found I had to fight hard to speak English on my return to England. I was quite literally *dreaming* in French! Madame was, I think, more impressed with my ability to set her hair in the then fashionable pin-curls when she was going out in the evening to dinner with friends, than that of nannying her little treasures, but complimented me regularly on my mastery of French so rapidly. I was always teased as being the one who loved "*les rues et les tripes françaises*", because I was able to pronounce the French 'u' like a true native, and my favourite dish was the French variety of *tripes* (not the honeycomb-tripe which was so popular with my Yorkshire family back home), cooked in a white wine sauce! Madame's maid, Christianne, was an accomplished cook working culinary wonders on a temperamental wood-burning stove.

No sooner had I returned home than I regretted doing so! Within hours Dad reminded me that I would not "sit around here being kept by him" and that he expected me to find alternative, instant employment in the UK! Wondering what on earth I could do with no qualifications whatever and seeming no nearer to taking further studies, despite my now fluent French, my mother accompanied me to the local government juvenile employment-bureau.

I felt very foolish and under-age at fifteen and a half, with nothing to offer *any* employer. My ex-French teacher, fully understanding the position, kindly suggested I might like to help a friend of hers sew quilts and eiderdowns in her home, but dress-making-lessons at school had produced one boring, hand-stitched Dorothy bag and a waist slip, plus a machine-sewn summer dirndl skirt and blouse, and I never sensed this was *my* forte.

Strangely enough, Dad had decided that I should become a shorthand-typist, but I never quite discovered how,

16

where or when, though presumably he hoped I would just 'pick it up' were I able to work in any office. Even so, there was a reference back to the canning-factory, and I was just bewildered and wanted to run away from *any* employment and give time to studying and qualifying. All this left me with a tremendous sense of rejection, inferiority and insecurity.

The interview with the juvenile employment-officer went far better than I could ever dare to hope. On discovering my ability to speak French fluently, plus the fact that I had been in an 'A' stream right through secondary school, I found to my amazement that at least *he* was not considering a canning-factory, nor, for that matter, *any* local employment whatsoever!

He asked me how I would feel about using my French in day-to-day work, but I was still having a problem wondering who would employ such an unqualified, uneducated individual! He then asked me, looking at my mother, whether I would be prepared to work in *London*! My mother was just smiling beneficently and was not at all antagonistic, but I was picturing Dad's face on hearing the glad tidings! "Well, I have flown to Geneva and back *all on my own*," I reasoned inwardly, "so what is a train journey of sixteen miles, twice a day?"

I dreaded telling Dad and, when I did, it was back to the pea-canning-factory line again. I just fled to the bathroom in sobs, but my mother came to comfort me and agreed to accompany me to London for an interview at La Banque Belge et du Congo Belge (Belgian and Belgian Congo Bank) which, in itself, sounded very grand and far beyond me! Obviously I knew nil about banking, let alone banking in Belgium and the then Belgian Congo! I had never darkened the doors of a bank!

The Personnel Manager of the Bank was such a friendly, middle-aged Englishman, who ushered my mother with much kindliness and fatherliness into an adjoining room where she could hear our whole conversation! He was very gentle and actually *wanted* my services in the Bank! He explained that I would start in the basement with filing and, little by little, climb the dizzy heights
of the banking-world. He added that basically promotion, and the rate thereof, was up to me, and for *all* this I would be paid the handsome starting wage of £2.12s.6d (£2.62½p) per week!

Overwhelmed with a mixture of trepidation and gratitude, I staggered out, leaving my mother to face the music when we got home, and to work out all the details as to *how*! To my utter dismay, Dad's initial reaction was, "You are not going to work in London! What's the matter with *here* anyway?" I dreaded this reference yet again, but Dad stopped in his tracks. Mum went to work on his better judgment, and came to encourage me and tell me that Dad had *offered* to lend me the money for my first monthly railway season-ticket, costing 25/- (£1.25), adding that I could pay him back *any time*, as I could afford it! Not only was it a startling and generous gesture - and an expensive one in 1951 for Dad, but he must have believed me capable of holding down a job for the first month, at any rate. Perhaps his idea of me being a shorthand-typist could be realised after all!

Shortly after this, we had all gone to bed one night, apart from Dad who was in the downstairs-cloakroom. Suddenly my mother heard crackling sounds and, on returning downstairs to investigate, she was horrified to find our sitting-room on fire. We did not realise at the time that this would be a recurrent

18

manifestation of Dad's pyromania in two different houses. Increasingly, he was also suffering from what is now called Post-Traumatic Stress after his experience as a prisoner-of-war under the Japanese. Of course, he blamed a spark from the fire or a cigarette-burn but, as time went on, we all knew differently. Fortunately we doused the flames successfully, with the speedy intervention of the Fire Brigade.

3. Study …. to Work (I Thess. 4:11)

My first real working-day dawned the following autumnal Monday morning. I felt extremely apprehensive, and it was all my mother could do to coax me to eat my cereal and half a slice of bread for breakfast, washed down with a cup of tea I had left to go cold. I had no appetite whatsoever. As she bade me goodbye at the front door, I wanted to run *anywhere* to escape! Work? Work? My whole being revolted, not against work for work's sake but I still felt so unprepared for the big, new world outside, the Metropolis and travelling alone by train. I knew no one and felt insecure, immature and useless. I still longed to study and take exams.

Somehow I got to the Bank, my thoughts in turmoil. A warm welcome awaited me and the members of staff were very friendly, some Belgian, some French, some German and many British.

A very kind, motherly soul handed me a ghastly navy blue, drill-overall, a starched, snowy-white, linen hand-towel, and a small tablet of cheese-like soap. I must have looked more like a convict in a women's prison than an employee of a bank-filing department, but *all* the ladies, apart from the Director's Personal Assistant, were dressed thus, as this was the Belgian custom them. These were, after all, still post-war years and, in fact, an overall can hide a multitude of sins, and save on wear and tear of personal clothing, of which I possessed an extremely limited, motley collection!

I was directed to the basement filing department, headed up by a jovial Englishman and his young, bachelor assistant, who very quickly had one-sided romantic notions about me! I finished my whole day's work by 10 or 10.30 and, within a short time, was transferred from there to a more up-market dossier section in the same basement, attached to a secretarial department. I also finished my work there by mid-morning and, as this section sported its own old, virtually unused manual typewriter, I decided to teach myself touch-typing in English and French with the aid of a text book.

I stayed at the Bank for just one year, as mounting to the promised dizzy heights of banking did *not*, as I had anticipated, appeal to me in the least. On reaching the ground floor - the banking-hall, which dealt directly with the public - where I was assigned the behind-the-scenes job of dealing with clients' stocks' and shares' certificates - I decided I wanted to climb no further! But by this time I had mastered basic typewriting with a medium speed in the two languages and planned, eventually, to add French and English Pitman shorthand skills thereto, once I was able to attend evening-courses. In fact, subsequent jobs all required me to type, and ultimately to cope with a full secretarial load and office-duties.

As time went by, I felt it was high time I began taking other subjects and examinations to make up for the enforced rest from formal education. I was, by now, living in bed-sits, mostly in London, and undertaking a full day's office programme and a couple of evening classes per week. I made a start by taking English and French 'O'-levels and passing both, the latter with flying colours, as it really was a cinch. Some of my jobs did not require a knowledge of French, so I kept this up by joining various evening French Circles

Next I went to work for a London firm of consultant-engineers. Here it was that I had my first real romance, apart from a fleeting one in France. Sadly, however, this man was already married. It all began innocently enough as I took my packed-lunch into the nearby park during the spring and summer months, where I discovered this work-colleague was alone doing the same thing. He was eleven years my senior, yet we had a lot in common. To a degree, he probably filled the missing father-figure in my life, and I found his stories about his home life, before he was married, very interesting. His father was a minister in what was obviously a rather high Anglican church. Religion intrigued me.

It was some time before I discovered this man was lonely and had rushed into a post-war marriage with a local girl, which proved something of a disaster. They had one baby daughter (and later a son) whom he idolised and whose daily progress was shared with me with much pride. Then there was the Christmas office-party, with drink flowing, and the inevitable pairing-up that tends to be the pattern on these occasions, culminating in our walking to the railway station together via one of those London cinemas that showed only short cartoon films and a news feature. I was, perhaps unconsciously, all too ready to gain a sympathetic ear and fall into welcoming arms. Too late! We seemed to have fallen hook, line and sinker, and it would take some years to go into reverse.

I respected this man's code of ethics, springing from both his family and church background, because he never expected me to enter into a full, physical relationship, which we both regarded strongly as being purely for married people. Nevertheless, try as we might on many occasions, we could not

22

stop seeing each other virtually every day, and spending as much time together as was possible on the pretext of working overtime.

I had unconsciously been searching for this mature affection, as he had for someone to show him love and respect, which he clearly lacked in his marriage. I met his wife at the office one evening, and saw at once that they were at complete opposite ends of the social scale and were totally unsuited, and therefore unable to communicate meaningfully.

It is possible that many such marriages were entered into as a result of demobilisation after the war. Direct involvement in wartime manoeuvres must work changes in people in the Forces, and also in potential partners left at home. Absence can make the heart grow fonder without a doubt, but transformation of character at differing levels can equally produce unbridgeable gaps, especially if one rushes into marriage.

It was while I was with this particular firm that I got into the habit of joining 'the boys' for an evening drink and soon became hooked on gin and orange, which helped me to drown my sorrows and guilt, at least temporarily. However, it is a well-known fact that its side-effect is depression, so it drowned one type of sorrow but led to other manifestations of melancholy.

When I realised how entrenched my friend and I were I tried to back out by leaving the company and working some distance away, but *that* did not work either! There was but one solution: I would try God! This man had Him somewhere in his background and, although his religion did not seem to be helping him in his marriage or daily life, or to break with me, surely God had to be *my* solution?

A friend who was still working at the Bank invited me to spend some weekends with her at her grandparents' home in Middlesex. She took me to her Anglo-Catholic church on the Sunday morning where I was out of my comfort-zone as none of my family attended church. In fact, they practised various forms of the occult without realising the dangers. I was, on the one hand, bored by the liturgy and sermon - in fact, I don't remember anything preached during the sermon - yet fascinated and drawn by what I can only now describe as the 'religiosity' of the whole event. In fact after that initial introduction I began attending church regularly on Sundays to try to salve my conscience, but continued to see my gentleman-friend on weekdays.

One of my job-moves was to the Regent's Park area of London, where I worked for a computer firm, which rented a terraced mansion with beautiful Adam ceilings in a very select area near to the BBC. One of my lady-colleagues, who had grown up in India, was Jewish. We have remained in touch ever since those far off days. This company employed a handful of Jewish ladies, but Joan was the one to whom I warmed the most.

An orthodox Jewish gentleman, who always wore the traditional skull-cap called a 'kippah' and came from Haifa, spent some months with the firm in order to study and write a thesis on some aspect of computers which this company manufactured. I had the privilege of typing for him. Much, much later, all this was to have an amazing significance in my life.

4. The Preaching of the Cross (1 Cor. 1:17-18)

There was a Billy Graham Crusade all about this time and, after the evangelistic appeal, I went forward, having recently been confirmed in a very high and dead Anglican church near my parents' home, thinking that I was now making a re-commitment to salvation - that I was already 'born again'. How I could have imagined that I was ever 'born again' is a mystery now, because there were no signs of spiritual birth, newness of life or the fruit of the Spirit. I was not even reading my Bible or praying regularly, and did not know how to set about it either. My life was full of compromise and worldliness.

Sadly, my confirmation, which had been preceded by weekly 'classes' in the vicarage, had no effect whatsoever on my life, and I deluded myself into thinking that Sunday genuflects and making the sign of the cross over myself would get me to Heaven. Nor could that meaningless ceremony give me the victory I craved over my love-affair - meaningless, that is, in *my* particular circumstances.

I must make it clear that I am in no way condemning confirmation services. Where there is true, prayerful, spiritual preparation and a person is definitely born again, that person may well, at that time, come into the fullness of the Holy Spirit, that being the *real* purpose of confirmation, of course. It was not, in fact, until Easter 1957, when I was twenty one, that I really came face-to-face with the challenge of personal salvation. Billy Graham preached a very fiery, biblical, appealing message earlier at Harringey, but I was not ready to allow it to affect my *heart* and the whole of my life. In effect, I was not ready to hand everything over to Jesus Himself and become a *new* creature.

I was living at home at that time, having only recently had a complete nervous breakdown, which was hardly surprising. On Good Friday I decided to practise good works and attend my parents' local Anglican church, where I had been confirmed earlier, for the three-hour Meditation on the Cross. I had not bargained for the lively, new, evangelical vicar who had come to replace the Anglo-Catholic one who had prepared me for confirmation, nor for his very challenging teaching direct from God's Word on the true meaning of the Cross. I saw, as if for the first time, with spiritual eyesight, that Jesus had died for *me*, for *my* sins, and particularly the sin of having an affair with a married man.

Somewhere halfway through those precious three hours, that seemed only like minutes, I knew what I had to do. I went home to my parents' house and, in the privacy of my bedroom, confessed my sins before the Lord, repented and asked Him to forgive and cleanse me and to grant me eternal life. *At once* I had an amazing peace and sense of being cleansed and accepted through the washing of Jesus' blood. I *had* now been born again; I *was* a new creature! I knew that it would be hard to testify first to my parents and then to my man-friend, in order to break our relationship and refuse to see him again, however much it may hurt both of us.

The Lord honoured my testimony and ultimatum and gave me complete victory, together with physical and emotional healing, and showed me He had other purposes for my life. I looked back over my first twenty-one years and saw clear evidence that the Lord had had His hand especially on my life since the age of seven when, after the loss of my father, I had really been searching for Something, Someone, The Truth. Interestingly enough, I had two childhood-friends, both practising Roman Catholics, one of whom hiked me off to the local monastery for Mass. I did not understand Mass or First Communion, but was absolutely enthralled by it all, and the processions with tiny girls dressed as little brides had me rooted to the spot. I had wanted to be such a bride, but my mother would not hear of such goings-on, yet was willing for me to attend services. She strongly disapproved of large Catholic families because they exercised no birth-control!

If I feared losing out because I had become a Christian, I was mistaken. Once the Lord got a firm hold of me, I lost precisely nothing and gained *all!* What amazing grace, mercy and patience God has!

So I became a follower of Jesus Christ. My parents sneered and jeered and said it would only last at the most three months, which only fired me with greater determination (or defiance!) to make it last a *very* long time! I was privileged to have the wise counselling and teaching of that vicar whom the Holy Spirit inspired to prompt me to take the step of committing my life to Jesus. Within nine days of my conversion, I was teaching a Sunday School class! This minister had unwittingly emptied the church of the Anglo-Catholics, churchy, bells-and-smells type members and, one by one, new people were coming in, drawn by an Invisible Force, and being saved! Likewise, one by one we were left to 'staff' the various church-departments, including the Sunday School. The Holy Spirit was so active that even the boys and girls were asking if they could give their lives to Jesus.

27

One Sunday morning, during Communion Service, this same minister suddenly turned away from the communion-table to face the congregation, only to be confronted by boy-servers, angelically clad in long, white gowns. Being an evangelical, he hadn't a clue what to do with any of them so, in his confusion, told most of them to get lost! Then somehow his foot caught the brass gong atop the chancel-steps which high churches sound at strategic points in the Eucharist. The gong descended every chancel step with an increasingly resounding '*boing*' and continued right along the centre-aisle, as he and we looked on with amused embarrassment and stifled giggles! That event put an end to servers, gongs and all high-churchiness once and for all, much to the minister's relief!

There were some seventeen adult people saved in a short space of time, all as green as grass and coming from very worldly backgrounds, but the amazing thing was that *several* were called independently by the Lord into full-time service. Some even became ministers themselves. Little did I know in those early days how the Lord could or would use *me* as one of them!

5. Go …. And Teach (Matt. 28:19, 20)

After handing my life over to the Lord and beginning to serve Him in the church through teaching Sunday School children, and learning so much thereby myself, attending weekly prayer and Bible study meetings, Sunday School preparation classes, helping in youth meetings, going to services and the after-church Sunday evening fellowship, etc., it came to my notice that the Church Missionary Society was staging a Missionary Weekend at another Anglican church in the area. Being at a loose end on the Saturday afternoon, I decided to go, being somewhat ignorant as to who or what a missionary was!

The Home Department of the Missionary Society had sent a couple of members of its staff to show a film entitled 'The Orange Tree', on the subject of the training of students at Mukono Theological College, Uganda.

I sat engrossed but was unprepared for what the Lord would do during its showing. Very, very clearly He called *me* to be willing to go to Africa to serve Him! I thought and hoped I must be imagining things, but then decided, were this *actually* the case, were He *truly* calling me to go, that I could, of course, never really *go* anywhere as a missionary, because my only profession was bi-lingual secretarial skills, "and He can't possibly need *those* on the mission field!" I argued with myself.

Eventually, after the film had finished, and while we were sitting having tea informally, I plucked up courage to speak to one of the two CMS staff present. I told him that I thought I must be mistaken, but somehow I felt God had called me to go to Africa to serve Him, adding hopefully that I supposed,

29

however, that no one ever needed bi-lingual secretaries or, for that matter, *any* kind of office staff on the foreign field. "Oh, that is where you would be wrong," he informed me, with a twinkle in his eye, "for we need *two* immediately!" I wished that the floor would open up and swallow me or that I could bolt for an exit-door, but the Lord had me nicely cornered!

My whole inner being shrieked, "Help, Lord!" I was still very young, physically and spiritually, having been a Christian for only six, short months. I was not ready yet. I needed more time, more in-depth experience of the Lord and knowledge of His Word, and to be generally older and wiser. But I have learnt that a command from the Lord to 'go', or 'do' often precedes a period of training and preparation, our obedience and willingness being tested initially when He gives the command, and it is a command, not an optional extra. My new evangelical background from the start contained the challenge to go, be, do, serve, but so much of today's Christianity never mentions serving the Lord and tends far more towards passivity and being spoon-fed and served than toward active-service, even at the home-end.

I have read of a number of missionaries who were soundly saved and called to serve the Lord as missionaries when they were in primary school. In the first book of Samuel, chapters 1-3, we have that lovely record of Hannah 'lending' her son, Samuel, to the Lord, in thanksgiving for the Lord releasing her from barrenness. The Lord took her at her word, and not only honoured Samuel's childhood-presence and -services in the House of the Lord, but quite independently called Samuel personally on three distinct occasions while he was still very young. God is no respecter of persons, nor of age.

I have come to see that God honours response and action when He calls, although that may also only be preparatory. I arranged over the next few months to have interviews with CMS and its sister-mission, the Ruanda Mission (later named Mid-Africa Ministry). Missionary Training College was mentioned for some stage in the future and I also enquired about other professions, despite the two recent vacancies for secretaries on the field! The traffic light was not red, but orange, so I began studying Pitman's adaptation-shorthand in French.

In the interim, after a year's study on the subject of water baptism from God's Word, prayer and counsel from a number of ministers from various denominations, I took the step of being baptised by immersion and, in fact, began attending a local Baptist church. This denominational change caused me to apply to the Baptist Missionary Society to work as a bi-lingual secretary in the Congo, but this was 1960 - the year that the ex-Belgian Congo gained its independence (prior to changing its name temporarily to Zaïre), and some of the lady-missionaries had come back to the UK due to a security-problem at that time.

I was invited to go and work at BMS headquarters near Baker Street, London, in the meanwhile, and had only just finished my French shorthand-course when an urgent call came from Léopoldville, the capital of Congo, as it was then. The Field Secretary of the BMS, Congo, had written saying that he was sending his present secretary home for medical treatment and needed an immediate bi-lingual replacement, who *must* be able to drive, on a three year, short-term contract.

I could comply with all the requirements except the last. How could I learn instantly to drive in order not to keep the Field Secretary waiting too long? I began lessons at once, but

31

could not obtain a test-date before I was due to fly to Africa in late December 1960.

In the depths of an English winter I had to rush around trying to buy 100% cotton clothing for the tropics. This was hardly the easiest time of year, as all summer-stocks were put away either for the January sales or for the following summer. However, I found small, private shop-staff very helpful and willing to clamber up ladders and get down their previous summer's stocks, and managed to purchase all I needed in the few weeks put at my disposal, interspersed with driving-lessons and obtaining gruesome vaccinations!

How 'co-incidental' it was that I had worked at La Banque Belge et du Congo-Belge in 1951-1952, eight years earlier, and learnt much that was invaluable concerning the colonial era and background to the Congo! *Nothing is ever wasted in God's economy!* Also it was in that very bank that I personally determined to become a fully-fledged secretary, and became familiar, even through filing or copy-typing letters, as to how the Belgians set out and phrased their correspondence. Then there were my five months in France prior to joining the bank, where I became fluent in French, Madame insisting I wrote *dictées* alongside her children! Just how far back did God begin preparing me for this hour? His Word tells me in Jeremiah 1:5,6 that *before* he formed me in the womb and before I was born He sanctified me and ordained me a prophet unto the nations! It is a mind-boggling, wonderful truth!

Long before my plane touched down in Brazzaville, ex-French Congo-Brazzaville, I was fascinated, as we made the descent, by the aerial view of minuscule, round, mud and wattle, thatched huts, with Africans going about their early morning

32

activities. A little earlier I had disappeared quickly into the wash-room to remove my winter skirt and cardigan changing into a yellow, cotton dress, as the plane's loudspeaker had announced that the outside ground temperature was 20°C, and it was still very early in the morning. This was my first long flight, and I had found it hard to sleep and to believe I was Africa-bound at last! My mother had been distressed at Heathrow, and I found it difficult to comfort and leave her.

As I was walking out of Brazzaville Airport, I heard a lady's voice calling my name! A senior missionary had come to meet and escort me across the ferry to Léopoldville, on the opposite side of the River Congo. I was surprised to see the river had so many beautiful water lilies growing in the water and my senior colleague explained that legend has it that these had been introduced by some well-meaning Belgian in colonial times, but that the lilies had become a great nuisance-factor to shipping, particularly to ferries and steamers.

The river is over one thousand miles long, and is very narrow in some parts while elsewhere it widens out to anything up to three miles, with many islands in between the opposing banks. The portion between Brazzaville and Léopoldville, and indeed the Baptist Missionary Society compound where I was to work and live, itself bordering the river bank, was only about a mile wide and one could see across to the other side quite clearly.

My colleague took me home to a delicious breakfast of paw-paw, cereal and toast served on her verandah overlooking the river, and then suggested I took some rest to recover from the journey, after which I might like to go to the BMS office a few yards further along the compound, where she had been holding the fort pending my arrival. I was exhausted, but my mind refused to switch off completely and I found it impossible to sleep, despite not having done so for many hours.

After a while I took myself to the office, where my gifted linguist-typist-teacher-colleague began explaining the inner-workings of filing and other office systems, but I am not sure I was capable of taking much in! However, the next day was Christmas Eve and she would not be able to spare any other time for handing over as she was spending the holiday with her missionary sister down-river.

The most formidable object in the office, believe it or not, was an *electric*, French-keyboard typewriter, whereas I was a trained touch-typist on a QWERTY *manual* English keyboard! This was the very last place I had expected to find an electric machine in those days, but 'Léo', as we called the capital, was modern and had electricity and running water - in theory, at any rate!

But one could *not* use the telephone if it was raining for fear of getting a shock! No one remembered to tell me this useful piece of information and it took me a long time to realise why, when telephoning the airport one very rainy day, the phone rang and rang the other end, and was finally answered by a man who picked up his receiver and replied with the abrupt comment, "It is raining!" ("Il pleut!"), and promptly put it down again. My silent response was, "Yes, I realise that only too well, but please ….!"

Another new missionary called Edna, who had preceded me to the field by a few weeks and was a school teacher, has become a lifelong friend and prayer-partner. She and I lived together for the first few months of my contract, and found we had the same warped sense of humour! We were given a kitten by some American missionaries, which we named 'Tweedy Harris' because that described the unusual combination of shades and markings on his fur. He was an absolute character, and kept us in fits of laughter some evenings as he rolled round and round our sitting-room inside a wicker waste-paper basket turned on its side! We were supposed to be doing language study and/or preparation for the following day's work, but Tweedy gave us regular evening entertainment to distract us from our duties!

Tweedy would go out regularly by day and hunt lizards, but had the callous habit of biting off their tails and then just leaving them, Manx-like, outside. One day the Vice-Consul visited the mission-office from the British Embassy. Tweedy had hidden behind a bougainvillaea bush, unbeknown to me, and, as I escorted this man to my flat for a cool drink, Tweedy suddenly jumped out, took one flying leap at the man's legs, all claws firmly dug into his trouser-leg, and continued to hang there as he walked, much to my shame and confusion! I began to offer profuse apologies and command Tweedy to get down, whereupon the Vice-Consul sardonically muttered, "Didn't know you kept lions around here!" I was most embarrassed trying, unsuccessfully, to peel Tweedy's deeply entrenched claws, including an extra ratting-claw on each paw, from this strange man's formerly immaculate trouser-leg and to persuade Tweedy to respect him for the VIP he was!

With Tweedy's claws fully embedded into his left knee and calf, the Vice-Consul began walking with a rather strange gait as he propelled the cat along in the direction of my flat. Then, quite abruptly, Tweedy responded to his internal-clock

35

and the fact that it was now time for his lunch, retracted all claws, jumped down, and without so much as a backward-glance or suggestion of apology, he trotted up the outside flat-stairway, meowing loudly for grub! Mercifully, I was able to shut him in the kitchen with his various saucers of milk and food, while I attended to the poor Vice-Consul. Tweedy frequently displayed jealousy if too much time or attention was devoted to visitors!

Many times, bang on the dot of noon, when I was supposed, theoretically, to go home for lunch and a siesta, Tweedy would come and rattle the mosquito-netting on the outer screen-door of the office. It was time for his lunch, even if I was busy, and he was going to be a thorough nuisance until I was driven to distraction! Alternatively, he took to hiding behind the same bush described in the Vice-Consul saga, and dash out, marching smartly ahead, with me bringing up the rear, as if I was incapable of knowing the way to the fridge where his milk was stored.

Food for humans was very difficult to purchase post-independence, let alone being able to find anything for a cat, with the exception of expensive Belgian meat, specially flown in for expatriates who had managed not to flee the country at independence. The BMS Medical Officer in London had stipulated that all missionaries working in Congo should eat as much Marmite as possible as a dietary-supplement, so it became a useful and economical source of food for Tweedy, when spread on crusts of bread. We could only obtain powdered milk, which had to be re-constituted every day and kept in the fridge and, when things were really scarce, we were forced to ship out tinned foods from England, which was an expensive business!

36

A fellow missionary down-river had been given a brother of Tweedy's, which she named Goi-Goi (lazy), and she decided to bring him to Léo to have him neutered. She and her cat stayed with Tweedy and me for a week, and the antics that pair of cats got up to were incredible, including hanging upside down on my French window mosquito-net shutters, playing tag, to see who would fall off first! Those shutters were not quite the same again, and hardly mosquito-proof after their combined claws had penetrated the wire!

The castration-operation on Goi-Goi certainly did not deter him from clowning, rendering his title something of a misnomer during that particular week, as he had every bit as much energy as Tweedy, who was also a neutered-male. We often wondered whether the whole, large litter was of the same ilk! Most of the eleven kittens had been given away to missionaries and, after all, it is said that animals take on their owner's character!!

The mission-office kept me very busy with French and English correspondence, answering the telephone, filing and coping with all the usual administration of a missionary society with many missionaries up and down river on a number of different mission-stations, most of them in bush situations.

In addition, I was invited to teach in the French Sunday school, attached to the Protestant Chapel near the mission-compound, where services were held in English and French. Also I became a youth leader of the Protestant youth movement, JEUNIPRO for which I had to drive some distance out of the city in a Battleship Grey Citroen 2 CV car, commonly nicknamed 'The Dustbin' (or La Poubelle), for that is what it resembled! In order to be able to drive solo, I had first, of

37

course, to pass a Congo driving-test, with a complicated theoretical, as well as a practical exam in French, and play 'dinky cars' around a model-track, on which nothing had been made to scale!

It was not easy to travel between mission-stations post-independence, as invariably the boats were 'en panne' (out of commission, due to lack of maintenance, missing parts, etc., and which we dubbed, perhaps more appropriately, 'in pain'). However, when I tried to travel by air, thinking this would be much quicker and more dependable, I was soon to learn the frustrations of going on safari in post-independent Africa.

The time had come for my mid-term leave and I was anxious to get away from the concrete jungle of modern Léopoldville which housed offices and rather empty shops. I decided I would like to visit missionaries in the Middle River area at Bolobo, where there was a hospital and a school. I was driven to Léopoldville Airport at the scheduled time, only to be informed at the check-in desk that there would be no flight today because there was no pilot to 'drive it'! It was casually suggested I try again tomorrow. I did just that, only to be told this time that the aircraft was on the tarmac, there was now a pilot, but that it had no door and could not fly without one! That factor, at least, was a relief!

Meanwhile, my holiday was quickly ticking by with no seeming chance of getting away that week. Suppressing frustration and impatience, a colleague drove me, once more, to the airport next day, and wonder of wonders, *everything* was intact! "Have pilot and door, will fly!!"

Having had to wait three days, I now had the added bonus of travelling right to Bolobo itself with a missionary-couple who worked there, who had pitched up in Léo in a Land Rover, amidst all this kerfuffle, and left the vehicle in the capital for repair. It was such a help having personal escorts, because one had to travel by canoe from near the little airstrip called Nkolo, and being fluent in Lingala, and knowing the people, they quickly secured the services of a reliable canoeist.

It was fascinating watching the skill of this man, as he steered the canoe, with outboard motor. Naturally, I was all agog for crocodiles but saw none! It was extremely hot on the open river in the heat of the early afternoon, and a tremendous relief, to arrive at last, and relax in the sitting-room of nursing-colleagues while sipping tea. I had come away extremely tired, and was more than ready for a complete rest, as well as taking a keen interest in the work of my up-river missionary-colleagues.

I was almost envious, in the nicest way, of what I had come to regard as 'true missionaries' - those who worked deep in the bush and lived and worked among the people of the country. In the capital, we were mainly engaged in serving the missionaries themselves, via essential mission-administration and, for the most part, we did not live in the midst of our African brethren. I felt this very keenly, but it was helpful to be assigned to one of the African churches on the outskirts of the city where, when a car was available, I worshipped only with Africans in Lingala and French, and my youth work was also all-African.

In those days I was somewhat squeamish about medical-matters, the sight of blood being sufficient to make my head reel and my body go comatose! I refrained, therefore, from taking up the suggestion to go and observe a live birth in the Labour Ward!

However, I used some of the holiday to good advantage when not resting, to get dug into some systematic language-study of Lingala, the lingua-franca or trade-language used up and down the Congo River. Being in an administrative post, I had little need to use this as my children's and youth work mainly required French, but I felt that I should be able to communicate more readily with church folk, many of whom were not very familiar with French, particularly the older women.

While on holiday, I also attended the Bolobo JEUNIPRO youth meetings, only to be invited to return to that station to take up full-time children's and youth work after furlough. A group of us also participated in a river-baptismal service some miles away, travelling by Land Rover. I was amazed how at home I felt deep in the bush. I loved all the sights, sounds and smells of food cooking over charcoal-braziers. There was a refreshingly keen commitment to the Lord in these bush-Christians. Also this was the first time I had observed river-baptisms and it was a most moving occasion.

The foundational language-lessons I was given during my holiday served to get me started once I returned to Léo. I was able to add to my knowledge little-by-little, as time was available, in order to translate for the first language examination. Sadly, I was never to sit that exam.

6. God Tests the Hearts and Minds (Ps. 7:9b)

In order thoroughly to familiarise myself with spiritual French terminology, it was essential to have my morning Quiet Time in French, using the Louis Segond translation of the Bible and then to pray *only* in French. I had not been in a francophone spiritual climate before so, while I could write and speak the language fluently, biblical phraseology was a new sphere for me! It's never easy to pray in another language.

Baptist missionaries who went to the mission-field on long term-service passed through the normal channels of missionary training college and then, if being sent to a French-speaking territory, spent time in Brussels, Belgium, following an intensive language course. In my case, there was not time for all this as I was to fill an urgent gap, but it did mean that I missed out on attending European Protestant evangelical churches where French was used.

During my second year on the field, it suddenly became 'popular' within the mission for ladies to go down with various forms of kidney-problems. I had had recurrent Malaria for some time, having a really bad bout every two or three months which left me very weak and lacking in energy. I seemed to be dragging around, with discomfort in my lower back and groin, so went for an appointment to a city clinic.

X-rays were taken of my kidneys, only to reveal that they were not really *plural* but joined in the centre by harmless fibrous tissue. The exceedingly impatient Belgian doctor told me that my kidney had 'dropped' and was not in the normal position at all, and that it would be better if I never returned to the tropics

41

again. I found myself thinking privately that that would be an excellent solution for *him*, there being no love lost between him and Africa nor, for that matter, his religious nursing staff or patients!

I was certainly having a lot of pain, and my private consultant in Congo recommended that any treatment be carried out immediately in Britain. I had very mixed feelings about leaving Africa for what appeared to be for good, but in all honesty was finding working for an ordained minister, forced into the administrative job of Field Secretary, very limiting. I was not really so much a secretary as a shorthand typist, since his wife opened all correspondence in her husband's absence and dealt with any telephone calls which went directly through to their house out of office-hours.

I have since realised that missionary-wives could, themselves, feel very unfulfilled and lonely. They could be easily subject to jealousy of single or other lady missionaries, and particularly any who worked, of necessity, in close proximity to their husbands. In no sense am I critical of this because a mission station set-up was a totally alien, abnormal way of life. I was by no means the first person to realise this and see that one needed to de-institutionalise a lot of missionary-work around the sixties and to live among the people wherever possible. There are pros and cons and, in so doing, one can lose out on close spiritual fellowship with one's own expatriate-colleagues.

Living among nationals can also be very noisy and disturbing, the average African having no concept of quietness and solitude whatsoever because most have been brought up in a large family in just one or two rooms. If the family is Christian, it is possible for *all* the members to pray aloud all at the same time, causing a regular but quite acceptable pattern into adulthood, and not minding at all who hears the content of their prayers! Nothing is kept secret in African society. Nevertheless, provided one is able to communicate fluently and accurately in the vernacular, it is very possible to have a deep, spiritual relationship with the national Christians, and this makes for less isolation and a more normal way of living.

So, in September 1962, I began to sell and pack up my few belongings and arrange for a trunk of household-items to be despatched to the UK by sea. Yet, in my heart of hearts, I did not really believe that I would never see Africa again, but at that stage knew nothing of the healing ministry which Jesus has offered to His people today.

It was inevitably hard to leave Tweedy Harris but Edna very willingly offered to look after him on her mission station in the heart of the Lower Congo bush to which she had been assigned. However, the incident earlier on with the Vice-Consul was to be repeated on others, with even more viciousness, until eventually she was forced to have him put to sleep. As a missionary she rightly felt that it was a poor Christian-witness to have a cat behaving like a wild animal and biting visitors, and I am in total agreement. One has to take the added precaution that such behaviour could be caused by rabies. If one contracted this disease it meant two weeks of very painful, daily injections into the stomach of anyone owning or having been bitten by a suspect-animal, and the very colleague with whom Edna later lived had already been bitten by another missionary's dog, which might have been rabid, and she had undergone such a course of injections

No sooner had I arrived at my parents' home than their doctor arranged for me to be hospitalised quite a long way away, as he felt I needed a London teaching-hospital with a well-known, experienced Renal Specialist. So I travelled in a church-friend's car all the way from my parents' home in Kent to St George's Hospital, Tooting, in South West London. Here I was to stay for a month's bed rest and have every conceivable test. Their X-rays and exploratory Laparotomy confirmed that I had only one kidney, or two joined by harmless, fibrous tissue, which may be prone to infection. The Specialist felt, however, that with rest and care I could soon be on the road to a full recovery. My diagnosis was, 'Has Horseshoe Kidney'!

No one made the comment that I should not return to Africa ultimately, and I found myself wondering why I had had to come all this way for such a confirmatory diagnosis. However, it is true that it is extremely difficult to rest and get away from work in a mission field-situation, and the intense heat of Central Africa. It would surely have been cheaper to fly to East Africa, although journeys and hospitalisation there all cost quite a lot of money. Also, because earlier that year I had unwittingly become emotionally involved with a Congolese youth leader with whom I worked, who asked me to marry him, it was propitious to get right away and take a complete break.

I never had any thought of marrying an African and, with hindsight, see that God did not intend me to do so, but that He had other plans for me much later on in this direction. However, it may serve some useful purpose to demonstrate how single missionaries living in the midst of older missionaries and missionary-couples can become very lonely, despite busyness, and therefore be caught off-guard and become emotionally

44

entangled with quite the wrong person, whether of their own culture or a foreign one, before they realise what is happening. Christian workers are very human and are just as liable to make human-errors as anyone else, the more so in overseas settings.

It is easy for Christians of the opposite sex, genuinely working, praying and sharing together in God's work, to become thrust together and to bond. It needs careful watching and, in some cases, totally avoiding. Sadly, in the case of some national pastors, it has even led to adultery and divorce through their quite innocently visiting lady-members of their flock. Getting to know each other spiritually through fellowship and prayer has sometimes opened the door for emotional-involvement and sin. I feel it is unwise for visitation on a one-to-one basis, and have counselled several young people to ensure that they go out two-by-two, as Jesus Himself commissioned.

During my time in hospital my great Aunty Amy, who had had a hand in my upbringing and who was now living alone in retirement near to my parents in Kent, had heard of a small, furnished flat that would be available for a year. My family felt I should rent this to give me time to re-orientate and settle in a job until I saw how things went with my health, they themselves hoping against hope that I would now "be sensible and stay in England!"

After four weeks in hospital, and as time grew near for my discharge, I confided in my Ward Sister that I felt too physically weak to move straight into a flat and rush around buying kitchen-equipment, etc. Sister was marvellous! I could say anything to her and, despite having a full ward and being run off her feet, she always spared time to listen. She had a word with the Almoner who arranged for me to convalesce in the Kent countryside for a further three weeks.

All this was in the middle of the very cold, snowy winter of 1962 when London had its first fall of sleet on 2nd October, and the snowfalls hardly abated until the following March! What a contrast to the very hot, humid temperatures of the Congo!

It seemed to take all my energy just to keep warm that winter, despite my flat being very well heated. In the early part of 1963 a local electrical-engineering firm, for whom I had previously worked in the late fifties, offered me a secretarial-post and it seemed appropriate to take it and not look for a bi-lingual job in London at that stage. I remember finding the climate, plus holding down a full-time job, difficult and exhausting at first but battled on, and eventually my former energy returned when the Spring months arrived. However, within a short time the firm merged with another, and the new bosses had a stroppy attitude toward some of the original staff.

I was sitting, with a fellow-secretary, in front of an upstairs-window which caught the full glare of the summer-sun, and asked politely if I might bring some curtains from home to hang up as sun-blinds. I had to ask one of the nastiest of the new bosses, whose office had the misfortune to adjoin ours, with a clear glass-partition overlooking our desks. He said he would consider it, but dismissed it deliberately from his mind at once. Eventually I appealed to the Company Secretary, whom I had known in the original firm. He was still responsible for staff-welfare and was more lenient, and he suggested I simply go ahead and hang the curtains, since they were mine and were not costing the company anything.

The curtains were duly hung early one morning before most staff had arrived, not out of secrecy but because hanging them involved climbing rather immodestly first on my desk-top and then onto the window-ledge. When the boss saw the curtains up, he demanded I come immediately into his office, whereupon he hurled accusations and abuse at me and telephoned down to the Company Secretary, with equal off-handedness. The upshot of this was that the Company Secretary lacked the moral courage to admit *he* himself was responsible for giving permission for the sun-blinds to be hung, and that secretaries could not be expected to type day-after-day behind the increasing afternoon heat and glare of glass panels without protection. Instead, he meekly obeyed the boss's whim that I be fired forthwith, purely on those grounds. My one week's written notice was simply worded, 'in the circumstances', and never stated a reason.

My colleagues were incredulous as they considered my work to be efficient, but nothing would change the tune of the surly boss who had come as the new boy into the company and was bent on throwing his weight around with the existing staff. Other personnel were also made mysteriously 'redundant' before and after I left. I had never had the sack before, but even *that* experience was to be used of the Lord much later on, because everything always is *in His economy*!

Fortunately, I was able to gain alternative work immediately in a firm producing electrical cables not very far from where I lived. When my flat lease expired, because it had been promised to the landlord's nephew and his new bride, the Lord provided a replacement-flat straight away, of the same size, even nearer my new company and my church. It was in rather poor decorative-condition, so I used a week's holiday to paint it. I realised that in re-decorating my flat I had passed a milestone in my health. I had enjoyed tackling this job and had not flagged once! The Lord's healing had not been instantaneous but it had been exceedingly progressive, and I was full of praise to my Great Physician.

7. Come Over... and Help Us (Acts 16:9b)

A close friend of mine, Jill, was in Kampala, Uganda, working as a secretary to the Church Missionary Society Field Representative. In those days, the four mission areas of Kenya, Uganda, Rwanda and Burundi were linked, as far as CMS and Ruanda Mission Field Representatives were concerned. Periodically, the representatives and their secretarial-staff got together to exchange news and views, and to fellowship and pray.

Such a gathering took place in 1964, and Jill was asked by the Representative of the Ruanda Mission responsible for Rwanda and Burundi (both countries coming under the Ugandan Anglican Diocese of Namirembe, Kampala, at that time) whether, by any chance, she might know of a bi-lingual secretary with French-English skills who would be free to act as a replacement for his secretary in Burundi, since she was leaving to get married.

Jill told him that she had such a friend but that there were two possible drawbacks: one, that I had already worked as a missionary in Congo but had been invalided home with kidney-trouble a couple of years earlier and, two, that I was a Baptist! Quite undeterred, the Anglican Field Representative, a medical doctor, said, "Oh, being a Baptist does not matter! We work very closely with Danish Baptists in Burundi anyway. The important thing is that she loves the Lord, is called and is now in good health!"

A blue aerogramme fell through the letter-box of the big house where I was renting my ground floor-flat. It had a Kenyan

49

postmark, and I could not imagine who could be writing to me from there because I knew no one in that country. The letter was from Jill (but posted by another missionary in Nairobi), warning me to pray and expect a letter from the Field Representative of the Ruanda Mission stationed at Buye (pronounced boo-yay), Burundi, not far from the Rwanda border, who was keen to secure my help. I was stunned but elated, having had a shrewd suspicion that my days in Africa were *not* ended after all and that my call from the Lord to serve Him there was not just for a short season. My health was good and had been stable for a long time. Even so, I felt quite unable to 'push open' the door to Africa myself but knew that, if that was genuinely the Lord's will for me, He would honour prayer and a willingness to return, and throw wide His door for me. I might add that such an attitude of patiently-waiting is quite contrary to my fleshly nature! For me to be passive is never easy, but I felt a definite restraint from Him, and it was mine to obey.

I called together seven trusted, mature Christian friends from my church, including my Pastor who, with his wife, was also a close friend and confidant, and asked them kindly to set aside a week to seek the Lord's face and will regarding my future. I left them alone to do this for seven days and then, one-by-one, they all quite independently confirmed that they were convinced it was the Lord's will for me to go to Burundi and that the final proof would be in my passing a medical-examination outright.

The Lord had led me to precisely the same decision but I felt I needed to submit to a group of elders to test whether I was on the right track, because it can be very easy to gain subjective-guidance. I had more than the scriptural requisite of 'two or

50

three witnesses', one of which should be God's Word, and He had certainly supplied that from Deuteronomy 11:10,12: "For the land, whither thou goest in to possess it, is not as the land of Egypt, from whence ye came out … But the land, whither ye go to possess it, is a land of hills and valleys, and drinketh water of the rain of heaven: A land which the Lord thy God careth for: the eyes of the Lord thy God are always upon it, from the beginning of the year even unto the end of the year." Burundi well-fitted such a biblical-description.

Interviews followed with the Ruanda Mission and the Medical Department of the parent-mission, the Church Missionary Society (both now renamed Church Mission Society and Mid Africa Ministry), who passed me as being A1 fit! These interviews were virtual repeats of those I had had some seven years earlier, shortly after my initial call to serve the Lord in Africa!

I was also invited to give my testimony at a Ruanda Mission Saturday afternoon prayer and fellowship meeting in Kennington, South East London, early in 1965. I was accepted as a Baptist but asked not to broadcast this fact among the Burundi Christians, among whom I would be living and working. Since I had been saved as an Anglican, Anglicanism was neither new nor strange to me, and a number of my friends had remained loyal Anglicans with whom I prayed and fellowshipped regularly, my friend Jill having been a case in point.

By the time I had given a month's notice on my flat and to my employer and packed my belongings in oil-drums and metal trunks, March 1965 was upon me. It so happened that another missionary from Buye was ready to return to the field at

51

the same time as I was due to leave and it was recommended that, since Marguerite was taking back a car, we sail together to Mombasa (Kenya), putting the car on board, and then drive through Kenya, Uganda, Rwanda and Burundi! How thrilled and relieved I was to have fellowship en route, and the privilege of such a long, interesting road-safari through four African countries!

While on board ship, Marguerite introduced me to the rudiments of Kirundi, the language spoken throughout Burundi (and in fact similar to Kinyarwanda, spoken in Rwanda). Kirundi was much more difficult to master than Lingala, I found, but it was full of linguistic challenge.

Marguerite was a very skilled surgeon and doctor whose gifts were greatly prized on the mission-field by Africans and missionaries alike. Not only were we to journey together, but we were destined to live together for the first year of what for both of us was our second term of service in Africa. She had long, slim hands, which not only made her a good surgeon but equally skilled as a dressmaker, cook and confectioner.

She had the privilege of owning a battery-operated record player, there being no mains-electricity at Buye then, plus a set of soothing, musical records. Whenever she saw that I was overtired, she would thoughtfully ask, "Would you like to borrow some music?" followed by, "The Sound of Music as usual, I presume?" How prophetic even those lyrics were to be, none of us could ever have guessed!

We worked in our different roles at Buye for almost four years, and then flew back together to the UK on leave just prior to Christmas 1968. I never did, in fact, work for the Field Representative who had originally written to me via my friend

52

Jill after all, as there was a delay between receiving his letter and my arrival in Burundi, but we met up in Nairobi in April 1965 on our way through Burundi. Meanwhile, his own plans had changed and he, his wife and missionary-daughter were going to the UK prior to the parents taking up a different appointment elsewhere in another African country. I believe this was all due to the Lord's overruling. Instead, I worked for his successor, a younger ordained missionary who, with his wife, had excellent linguistic gifts and both were very musical. He was very clued up on administrative-procedures, yet always humbly open to listen to any suggestions I had to make as to possible improvements or short-cuts.

My main work was very similar to that in Congo but with more scope and freedom to include other spheres of service. I was press-ganged into teaching Sunday School in Kirundi after only *six months* of being on the field! Kirundi is a pure *Bantu* language with ten different classes of nouns. (The term '*Bantu*' refers to a large group of African Negroid races and their type of language. The actual word means 'people' so a Bantu language literally means 'the language of the people'.) My first, stumbling Sunday School lesson-notes were *read* from the back of my flannel-graph board or biblical picture, held in such a position as to enable me to glance at my vocabulary list! But it did wonders for my fluency, and I was so grateful afterwards to my senior colleague's-wife for plunging me into teaching in the vernacular!

Another area of teaching was in the hospital, where I was asked by the missionary sister-in-charge if I would teach the nurses French, since all their training notes were in that language by government law. I greatly enjoyed my twice-weekly contacts with male and female medical assistants and nurses in training, and taught them a French carol to sing in church one Christmas.

My greatest sense of fulfilment came when I was invited to teach the pastors' wives, whose husbands were training for the ministry at the Buye Theological College. Some women could not even read and write when they first came, but another missionary held literacy classes and it was not long before we began to see positive results. I taught them New Testament and Doctrine, with a little Gardening and Cookery.

At this stage I was living alone in what was known as 'Flame Tree Cottage' named after the beautiful, big flame tree with orange blossoms in season, in its front garden. The soil was very rich and fertile at Buye and, being at an altitude of 6,000 feet above sea-level with excellent rains and in such a southerly position, I was able to grow almost all varieties of fruit and vegetable known both in Africa and Europe.

One thing we all grew in our gardens like weeds was Spinach and, one gardening lesson, I invited all eight of the student-wives to come and help themselves to roots of it to transplant into their own gardens. They just could not believe that the soft, tender leaves would be cooked and ready to eat the way they liked it in just eight minutes, because most African green vegetables are fibrous and tough, and take much longer than that to cook. (Obviously, the boiling-point at an altitude of 6,000 feet above sea-level would vary from that in the United Kingdom.)

I showed the women how to make spinach and mixed-vegetable soup, and impressed upon them the strong iron content of the spinach and how good it was for their children. They were all convinced, and each college garden contained a mass of spinach in the rainy season from that day forward. And their families exuded good health!

The hospital decided to take on a Murundi secretary and I was asked to teach him to type. Having started to do so, I found a stream of others also interested in learning office-skills, including several missionaries! I began holding one general evening class a week, and then the Bishop asked me if I could hold actual commercial courses for church workers from the whole of the Burundi Diocese (now independent from its original Ugandan one). I agreed wholeheartedly, but almost regretted it when I discovered that some students had procured French keyboard-typewriters while wanting to do their coursework in either French, Kirundi or English, while others had the QUERTY English keyboard and wanted to do their coursework in anything but English, resulting in me nearly standing on my head trying to teach them all in *one* class!

I was by this time fluent in Kirundi and had passed my first language exam so, by mutual consent, I gave all class-directions in the vernacular and then individual tuition on a one-to-one basis, adapting as we went along the French textbook I had duplicated. I used to bang the theological college-drum to encourage rhythm-typing and to motivate speed and, amazingly, it worked!

The Diocese, and the Bishop in particular, felt I had a gift for teaching and invited me to return, after furlough, to full-time teaching, concentrating primarily on commercial courses for church-workers. How gracious is our God! *Me* teaching? The ignoramus of 1951 who longed to do further education and read French at University but never had the privilege had, since then, attended God's college of further learning, with His Word as my main textbook and His leading and experience day-by-day in His school of life and prayer. I never cease to wonder at His patient training, moulding and gentle rebukes as we avail ourselves, green as grass, for use in His service. He is not so much looking for educational degrees, it would seem (although today's governments quite understandably are), but willing, open hearts. Yet there were still so many rough corners for Him to smooth! I guess there always will be this side of heaven.

It was not uncommon for typewriters needing repair to be 'walked' atop an African head from quite a distance, African logic being that if one could operate a machine, one would be able equally to repair it! Most needed a good clean and a spot of oil, but I found the Lord to be an excellent Master Mechanic who is able to show one of His children how to repair what is needed for His work. By the same token, I was enabled to take the mission-duplicator to pieces and wash its silk-screen in soapy water in order to rid it of congealed ink, before the Lord supplied a new, more modern version. We also learnt to pray over faulty office-equipment, recognising the enemy's expertise at throwing spanners into the Lord's works.

Office-machinery presents a number of parabolic parallels to the Lord's dealing with His children. It is often only when we are in a state of disrepair that we come to Him, the Master Mechanic, for cleansing, repair and the oil of His Holy Spirit. Our lives can be very congealed with sin and very, very gently He may need to take us apart in order to heal old wounds and scars from yesteryear. Some parts may have to be scrapped forever for they are no longer relevant to the new, spiritual life, while others may need sand-papering before they can be lovingly replaced. Out from His heavenly store-room may need to come

56

brand new, shiny spares. Each of us has different needs but, whatever they may be, our great God has everything we need to enable us to function, serve and witness for Him.

A few months before leaving for furlough, the Lord had become doubly precious to me. I had gone on holiday with a friend called Linda who was a missionary-nurse working in Rwanda. We drove to Kabale in South West Uganda - one of my favourite holiday spots. We spent some time on Lake Bunyoni - a lake that is more than 6,000 feet above sea-level and extraordinarily beautiful. We had prayed about which book of the Bible to read as a study-background during our holiday and both arrived at the same conclusion: the book of Acts. For some time I had heard of those who were being 'baptised in the Holy Spirit' and Linda was one such person. I longed to ask her a hundred questions, and she prayerfully prepared herself to answer them from her own and others' experiences. I knew that I lacked spiritual power in my service for the Lord and that there were areas in my life that needed His deliverance from bondage, stemming both from my inheritance and all that I had contracted during my then thirty two years.

We read how Jesus had appeared after His resurrection and promised His disciples in Acts 1:8, "But ye shall receive *power* after that the Holy Ghost is come upon you: and ye shall be witnesses unto Me both in Jerusalem, and in all Judaea, and in Samaria, and unto the uttermost part of the earth." Then we continued to read in Acts 2 how, on the day of Pentecost, a mighty, rushing wind had come upon the early church, and there appeared cloven tongues of fire above them and "they were filled with the Holy Ghost, and began to speak with tongues, as the Spirit gave them utterance." Yes, that was exactly what was lacking, I acknowledged to myself, as we sat by the lakeside.

As we read on day-by-day, with me asking question-after-question, I desired this infilling of, or baptism in, the Holy Spirit with all of my heart and was determinedly seeking the Lord to obtain it. He showed me many things that were wrong in my life: attitudes, relationships, reactions, etc., and I brought each one to Him with repentance for total cleansing and forgiveness, and had His assurances that He had put these behind His back once and for all. I knew too that, when I got back from holiday, I must actually see a number of my colleagues and ask their forgiveness for many things I had thought, said and done, and also forgive them for things I held against them, irrespective of whether they changed and asked me to forgive them or not. I was amazed at how slow I had been to learn but praised the Lord that this in-depth study of the experiences of the early church was working in me a profound conviction, and that cleansing had to precede the Lord's infilling by His Holy Spirit. He has to fill a void, not a rubbish-heap of besetting sin!

On our way back from holiday, and as we went deeper and deeper into the book of Acts, we had to spend a couple of days on a mission-station in Rwanda before picking up lifts back to our respective stations. It was during this time, when totally alone in a missionary family's guest-room, with Acts 2 open on my bed, that I took by faith the words of the Psalmist in Psalm 81:10(b), '... open thy mouth wide, and I will fill it' and claimed this promise for myself by faith, in the name and power of the risen Lord Jesus. Immediately I felt a tingling sensation in my mouth, then sounds and syllables were issuing forth from my tongue! Not unusually, because I studied and spoke three languages other than my mother-tongue, I made the mistake of trying to analyse what I was speaking, and with that fleshly analysis came inevitable doubts. "It did not *sound* like a conventional language," I argued with myself and, therefore, with the Lord!

However, I persisted in using my tongue and it became increasingly fluent as I went on. Sometimes it appeared that I was worshipping and praising, or praying with intense burden in intercession, while on other occasions I seemed to be battling with the works of darkness with genuine and permissible righteous anger, as the enemy sought to build his satanic kingdom within God's domain.

After returning to my mission-station in Burundi and putting things right with a number of missionaries and African brothers and sisters, people began asking me what was different about me. I realised I must have been pretty awful before, and was still very far from being where the Lord truly wanted me! Previously it had been mission policy to keep such experiences private, but here were people noticing a difference without my actually telling them. In the end I was forced to spill the beans, only to find that some colleagues had already received the baptism of the Holy Spirit, with several more going on to do so, until ultimately most on the field had the same blessed experience. The Lord was beginning to effect changes in us all but this was, and always is, only a genesis.

8. Things Which God Has Prepared (1 Cor. 2:9-10)

After returning to the UK on leave and spending Christmas 1968 with my family, who by now had retired to the Kent coast, I moved to North London. Early in the New Year I visited my old college - Pitman's Central College, London - and to my amazement and delight they offered me a free-facility scholarship, both to observe lessons given by their staff to pupils and for me to study any sphere I wished for up to a year, provided that I financed any examinations I may wish to sit there. This was exactly what I needed to prepare me to become a fully-fledged, certificated teacher of typewriting, so I could return to Africa with added bona fide credentials.

I set to work at once, observing and making notes and, at the same time, refreshing my own skills. I also enrolled for the teachers' evening-class and took qualifying typewriting examinations, in order to study for two teacher-of-typewriting examinations the following Spring (1969). While I was at it, I decided to sit some French exams also, to keep my hand in, and in seven months had taken a total of twenty two papers, mainly in these two subjects, with a view not only to being more qualified but possibly to using such examination-papers for students in Burundi.

"So, dear Lord," I recollected in thanksgiving around this time, "You have seen to it that I studied languages in Your university, and have qualified me to be a teacher by Your miraculous provision and intervention, after all. Your ways, O Lord, are past finding out, and I marvel and give it all back to You. Do with me and it whatever and wherever You desire."

60

The College also employed me as a Teacher of Typewriting during the summer months of 1969, for which I received a small salary, prior to going to Bible College as suggested by the Ruanda Mission. There had been no opportunities previously, because my secretarial services were always required in a hurry on the mission-field to fill urgent vacancies. However, it had always been an unfulfilled desire to take a year out and study the Bible full-time, but in fact I was only able to secure an educational grant if I were willing to undertake a two-year Diploma in Theology course, set by the University of London. But this subject was really not for me!

I do not wish to be critical in any way of those who have found theology helpful and could cope, but for me it was destructive of the scriptures trying to fit them into such categories as deutero- or tritero- Isaiah, meaning that this prophetic book had such markedly differing styles and approaches that it must have been written by more than one author. I did not seem to have the kind of mind or personality that frankly questioned who had written it, or in which style, but the simple faith and contentment that it had been written by one of God's servants and was meant to be part of His anointed Word. For me it was full of prophetic meaning and spiritual richness, and that was enough! That may sound simplistic but, by the time I had battled for five months over one main question for my examination, as to whether the book of Daniel was written in the second or sixth century and how this could be proved, I knew it was time to throw in the sponge with 'defeat', but with my faith intact!

In the Diploma of Theology course we had to study Greek, which totally baffled me. A dead language, dictated to us

61

at around 120 w.p.m. was, to me, a complete bore and waste of time. But it was also very good for any lurking linguistic-pride I may have had that I could not master Greek, but rather that it had mastered me! However, I have a genuine interest in what the original biblical text actually means, with all its nuances, whether Greek or Hebrew.

I still had some work to do on two external examinations while attending my London-based residential Bible College, which meant an exceedingly full academic programme alongside the essential DIY domesticity and college secretarial help, to keep costs of training as low as possible. All this proved too much, and my health went down very speedily once more with kidney symptoms.

In my second term I began haemorrhaging while staying in a friend's house, and again while with my parents during the holidays. It was quite obvious that I must rest, and had to take a huge chunk of time off from my course before I was sufficiently well to continue at college. My Principal was most understanding and said she wished others who could not cope for health and other reasons had the courage to back down, because some of the other students were having breakdowns but trying to soldier on. She was happy for me to continue for one more term just following the General Course plus taking my turn at domestic-work, and those final months were very manageable and blessed, with all the pressures off.

How easy it was to feel an utter failure at first, but I now know that theology (which the Oxford Dictionary defines as 'science of religion' and which some Christians term 'man's idea of God') is simply not my cup of tea. I may have taught in a theological college overseas, but arguments and discussions, and the pulling of God's Word to shreds, hold no interest for me. My faith may be simple, but I have proved God and His Word as being true and faithful for so long that a purely academic approach is neither helpful nor appealing in that sense to me personally. And theology bores me to tears - for me it is so empty and unreal!

It would be useless pretending that going to Bible-college after two terms on the foreign-field was easy. Being in my early thirties by this time I was, on occasion, taken for a member of staff by visitors! But however young or old, physically or spiritually, none of us can ever say that we have nothing more to learn. Sadly, most of us remain at the bottom of the class learning spiritual truths for far too long. Even after being promoted to the next class, we often need to return to the foundational truths again because the Lord shows us we are not living them out in our daily lives. How patient and merciful is our God, Who does not give up on us, nor condemn us, but justly and lovingly corrects us, His wayward lambs!

After leaving Bible-college in the summer of 1970 I took a bedsit in Twickenham, Middlesex, in the house of Christian friends of an ex-missionary friend of mine, and set about finding work. I was still having recurrent problems with my kidney from time to time, so it was not possible to make any plans for returning to Africa as yet. By a wonderful 'God-incidence', my landlord was a Renal Consultant at a London teaching hospital and he introduced me to his senior colleague who put me on a high dose of a sulphonamide, which very successfully knocked the infection on the head once and for all.

I now needed to work again and would have liked to teach typewriting, but the salary was so abysmally low and it was necessary to become financially solvent after a year at Bible College.

A post was advertised in the local 'rag' for a Supervisor of a typing-pool in the Social Services Department of a London borough council. I applied, was offered the job, and the work proved interesting yet heartbreaking, because we were responsible for typing the Social Workers' reports. Child abuse was rampant in that area, as was illegitimacy and every form of social problem. I well remember one case-report on a couple who were living together who had two children but on their social security claim-form had fabricated the names of two more non-existent children, with supposed dates and places of birth. When the Social Worker called on them and asked for further evidence of these extra offspring, the woman quite casually admitted that they had not yet been born but, when they were, those were the names they intended to give them!

All of the Social Workers and other staff were very easy to relate to but there were problems in the higher echelons of staff. One man perpetually harassed me by demanding that I come in early every morning to do his secretarial work before other staff arrived, which was certainly not part of my contract. Here was a common case of expecting Christians to be doormats and take no corrective action!

Eventually I was forced into a corner and, after much prayer, the Lord showed me that He had not actually led me to this post and had never, in fact, called me out of full-time service. I was justly humbled, repented before Him and sought His cleansing, and left the Council as soon as my notice had been worked. I was puzzled, however, as to how He meant me to serve Him full-time, until I was waiting on Him one day prior to leaving the Council and He spoke almost audibly. "CMS", He said! It seemed He was leading me to go to the Church Missionary Society headquarters to serve Him there, but in what capacity? Was I imagining things?

My responsibility began by making an appointment with the Personnel Officer, not quite certain in what manner I was supposed to serve, but I decided to take my teaching and other typewriting certificates with me anyway, only to discover during my interview with him that the Society urgently needed a Supervisor for their typing-pool. An ex-missionary nurse had been filling the gap in that department but had just resumed hospital work.

When the Personnel Officer saw that I was a qualified teacher, he felt there was added scope for teaching junior-typists employed at headquarters in order to upgrade their knowledge and potential. I was, therefore, appointed to fill these two roles almost immediately, and a blackboard was fitted to the wall behind my desk for use in lesson periods, which were twice a week for forty minutes each, during the morning-hours.

It was absorbing and fulfilling work as one of the key jobs was to type and check stencils of missionaries' prayer letters, so I was kept very closely in touch with what was happening on various continents, including Africa. We were also responsible for all the Information Department's photocopying and typing of Press clippings of news affecting the Society's fields of work, and much else besides on the Home Department end. I felt I had come full circle as I looked back to the CMS missionary-weekend some thirteen years earlier when the Lord had first called me to serve Him, and my asking ex staff

65

members of this same CMS Home Department if the Lord actually needed secretaries on the foreign field!

During this period in my life, I found myself praying the oddest prayer that I have ever prayed. But the words proved not only to be those the Lord gave me, but which He intended to answer in the days ahead. I now realise that I was, in fact, praying prophetically.

To my amazement, I found myself asking the Lord for a husband ten years my senior, even a widower, with at least two children and a missionary-calling to Africa so that we might minister together, who was baptised in the Holy Spirit, etc, etc.

"But how very peculiar," I reflected immediately afterwards, as I silently reviewed my spiritual shopping-list. "Why should *I*, of all people, be asking the Lord for a husband when long ago I came to terms with the single-life and had now begun to climb to the top of two professions, and had become very much 'the career-woman'? After all, I was already thirty four and the chances, humanly-speaking, would be very slim," I mused to myself. Then very quickly I reminded myself that the Lord never dealt in human terms because He was the Lord Almighty, and that 'prophetic praying' eliminated anything remotely human or even logical, according to man's understanding. I prayed that strange prayer but once and then went about my daily life as normal, temporarily forgetting all about it!

One bitterly cold November Sunday evening that same year (1970) I felt very strongly impressed to turn out of doors to attend Evening Worship at my local Evangelical Anglican church - St Stephen's of Twickenham. I had gone 'all Anglican' again because it was the liveliest church in the neighbourhood, as far as I was then aware, very open towards the baptism of the Holy Spirit and beginning to move in greater freedom of worship.

The Vicar had previously had a living in the Anglican Church of Nakuru, Kenya, so was also very missionary-minded. In addition to this, I was now working with an Anglican missionary-society at the home end, and it all made for a less bitty and confusing approach to spiritual expression if I stuck with one denomination! I certainly was not aware of any Baptist church within walking distance, in any case.

However committed I was to the Lord and His House, I thought I must be crazy to go out on such a freezing night, but felt compelled to do so. We had the usual good, challenging sermon and, just as I was leaving the church-porch after the service, the Vicar caught me by the arm and steered me towards a man standing outside the church-door, all muffled up in a thick sheepskin-coat, Trilby hat and sheepskin-gloves. "I would like you to meet John," said Martin, "who lives and works in Kenya, and I think you would have a lot in common to chat about while I just finish up in the vestry."

I did not have a sheepskin-coat on and was desperately cold and longing to get back to my warm bedsit. John introduced himself more fully as, "I am John Fulcher and I live in Nakuru with my wife and family. We are serving the Lord full-time, and you?" I supplied my name and added I had worked in Congo and Burundi for a total of nearly six years and hoped to return to the latter some time the following year. We discussed people and places we knew and shared on spiritual matters affecting East Africa, but I began to wonder what had happened to Martin and just how much longer he would be, so that I could go home! He and his Treasurer must have been counting an extra generous offering that night!

John was also baptised in the Holy Spirit and, realising I was too, he asked if I knew of a local, weekly charismatic house-fellowship, which I did not, and he suggested he collect me the following Tuesday evening in his car, as he had almost to pass my door to drive to the meeting.

I readily agreed, although this was my first meeting of this kind, and I have to admit to being taken aback slightly by a number of bearded young men greeting ladies attending the meeting with a 'holy kiss'! I remember physically flinching, and the brother welcoming arrivals at the door taking the hint! After all, we had never met! I was somewhat relieved that John, at least, was not going around kissing strange women on the cheek but, in true British, stiff upper-lip fashion, was shaking hands at arm's length, like me!

The meeting was very 'free' and, for the first time, I witnessed dancing in the Spirit, the gifts of tongues, interpretation and prophecy, etc, although in that era could not necessarily have identified all of them so precisely. Amazingly, when I got into the large sitting-room where the meeting was to be held, who should I see but my ex-missionary friend Peggy, who had owned my cat's brother, Goi-Goi, in Congo! How astounded we were to be meeting in such different circumstances, having not seen each other for over eight years and having lost complete touch, yet we discovered that we were now living in adjacent towns in the UK! The Lord had, in the interim, met with us in very similar ways spiritually, and blessed us with the fullness of His Holy Spirit.

We visited each other's homes thereafter although I did not, in fact, return to that house-group, being sufficiently committed to services and meetings in my own church, plus attending a weekday evening French Circle. But apart from all that, I was not yet ready to be quite so free!

John ran Peggy and me back home at the end of the meeting and he invited me to join him and his wife for supper the following week. They were renting one of the Foreign Missions' Club flats in North London during their short UK leave, so I arranged to go over by Tube straight from the office one evening the next week.

Again, John kindly met me by car and drove me the few minutes' journey to the flat. He introduced me to his wife, Jane, and the smallest of their four daughters, Louise, aged three and three-quarters. The older three girls had been left at boarding-school in Kenya and were expected to join their parents for the Christmas Holidays in London.

After supper, and helping Jane to dry the dishes, Louise was put to bed and we sat in the sitting-room for a time of fellowship and prayer. Much to my surprise, while we were praying together, I had a clear, visually illustrated word of prophecy for John and Jane concerning their return to Kenya in the New Year, yet none of us had a lucid interpretation.

I saw a mass of water, with two very green plants growing beside it whose roots went down deeply into it. One plant bore a single, beautiful flower, the petals of which faded, dropped to the earth and died, but the stamen remained intact. Where the petals had fallen, fruit began to spring up in their place. The prophetic message which accompanied this vision was simply this: "I send you forth as two green plants, planted by a waterside. One will bring forth a single, beautiful blossom. That flower will soon fade, its petals fall to the ground and die but, where they fall, much spiritual fruit shall be borne."

"What a funny picture," I thought to myself, and doubtless John and Jane were thinking something similar, "so positive, yet it includes fading, dropping and dying?" I understood plainly enough what was meant by the two green plants, for here were two servants of the Lord who had been saved in the colonial-era in Kenya and whose spiritual-roots had gone quickly and deeply into God's spiritual-water, through a profound study and understanding of His Word and a life of prayer, often with fasting.

I had not recollected that they lived near to the large Lake Nakuru almost in the centre of Kenya, and that that too was a beautiful, physical mass of water. Later, we were to realise why the rest was to remain an enigma … However, these words were first confirmed by Psalm 1:1-3 and John 12:23-26. Interestingly enough I discovered, much later, that both these portions had been marked in red in Jane's own Bible!

Jane was very unobtrusively expecting her fifth baby, but I did not know this and it was not mentioned at all in conversation. John and Jane had met in Nakuru in the late fifties and they married in 1959. Jane's ambition was to have a large family of six children as she loved babies but basically preferred baby girls, probably because she was a most skilled dressmaker and enjoyed making frilly dresses! John had married when already into his thirties and was not keen to have more than a total of two children and always hoped at least one would be a son. However, up to the time I met the family, it had been girls all the way, and four of them at that!

70

I did not see this family again as they attended a UK Prayer and Bible Week in the New Year of 1971 and then returned to Kenya, but we exchanged addresses and kept in touch periodically. At that time I had no definite idea as to if or when I would be returning to Burundi, but thought it unlikely we would meet again.

As winter turned to spring that year I felt a clear stirring in the May from the Lord to make preparations to return to Africa. I had received a specific ministry of healing when an American lady minister was visiting my church and she had two words of knowledge concerning me, although we had neither met beforehand nor talked. These were: association with the occult, and what she termed 'a death wish' (or suicidal tendency).

The first I could see and acknowledge at once, stemming from my family on both sides, but the second was a mystery to me. She had named the latter almost as a postscript, just as she began turning to another person kneeling at the altar-rail for ministry. My mind was an utter blank and I could not, at that moment, ever recall having wished to die. As I was returning home I prayed all the way for the Lord to show me if I had ever desired to commit suicide. The heavens seemed as brass!

At 04.45 the following day I was awakened as if by a sharp hammer-blow. I saw a very strong, bright light at the foot of my bed and sat up with a start. I knew it was the Lord Himself, and He said, "When you were a child …"

"When I was a child, Lord?" I echoed, "What happened then?" Immediately before me was a picture of a childhood scene. My mother had taken me to a fortune-teller's house in order to have her own future told, when I was at primary school. I saw myself sitting afraid and uncomfortable on the edge of an

71

upright chair, wanting to escape anywhere. So yes, of course, this was what that American lady minister had been shown by the Lord the evening before. "Yes Lord, I remember now!" I told the Lord and myself, for within a few days following this childhood-experience, true enough, I had wanted to commit suicide.

At that time in my childhood I was still grievously mourning the loss of my father, and my best school-friend, Jennifer, was equally mourning the death of her beloved dog, a Cocker Spaniel. We schemed together to take poison but, out of cowardice and compromise, I watered down the rheumatic-emulsion from my Aunts' bathroom cabinet. Nevertheless, drinking this concoction made me very ill and produced the first kidney symptoms I was to have. There I lay on our settee, with most of our sitting-room windows blown to smithereens by a Doodlebug which had dropped a day or two earlier at the end of our road, killing one person and knocking two semi-detached houses as flat as a pancake. The doctor did not seem to detect any attempt at taking poison, and diagnosed Nephritis. It was not until much later that I myself saw any connection between that event and the consequent illness. Its roots were in the occult.

As soon as I received this confirmation from the Lord all those years later, repented and asked Him to forgive and cleanse me for seeking, as a child, to take my own life, I set about getting ready to go into the office early enough to type a letter to the lady who had ministered to me, with a copy to my vicar, making a full confession. This action was to release total and complete healing to my kidney and deliverance from all the memories, grief and actions associated with occult involvement.

The fact that it was my mother who actively visited a fortune-teller did not absolve me from its deep and ongoing effects, nor from my personal repentance for my sin committed in ignorance, with no alternative. (Compare Leviticus 4.)

After this, I was able to reduce the sulphonamide to a fraction and then come off it altogether, much to my relief and praise to the Lord for all He was doing. It should not be overlooked that in going to Africa, which has a constant background of witchcraft, ancestor-worship and other various forms of the occult, it is very easy to get into bondage in this realm, passively, without at first realising it. Any quarrel with a worker, for example, can and does lead often to him putting a very real curse on you, sometimes involving the local witch-doctor. Anyone going to Africa (or for that matter most other continents) as a Christian needs to be well aware of this danger.

Jane's fifth child was born on 30th May 1971 - Pentecost Sunday - although quite unknown to me at the time. To everyone's surprised delight this baby was actually a *boy* at long last! It was during this very same time that I had felt I must prepare to return to Africa, with a strange sense of urgency.

During the same month of May I went to Brussels to research methods of teaching secretarial-skills in French (as opposed to Flemish). I had used a Belgian system while in Burundi and wanted to see this demonstrated first-hand. The institute in question was extremely helpful and the Director's wife and staff were most kind and co-operative in permitting me to observe classes and talk to them and their students.

The typewriting-teacher introduced me to a Murundi girl who was studying under her tuition and, to my amazement, she turned out to be the niece of a man I had known quite well in

Burundi who had, at one time, been quite high up in government-circles. She was so thrilled to see me and we spoke together in Kirundi. I shared with her that I was staying at an evangelical Bible-college, explained where it was, and invited her and her uncle to join us a few days later for a house-group Bible-study in one of the staff apartments.

The uncle greeted me like a long-lost missionary, and insisted that I make immediate arrangements to return to Burundi in order to teach secretarial-skills once more, offering at the same time to do all that was necessary to ensure that permits and an unsalaried post were available. However, I learnt to my dismay that the job he had secured was as a fill-in head of a school, for the first year, after which I was expected to be released to offer secretarial skills' courses to the various church leaders and members in his country!

I protested as graciously as I could that I had never worked in a school-posting before and was neither qualified nor capable of taking on a headship, but nothing would diminish his determination to get me back in Burundi after an absence of two and a half years. He simply could not see what possible reason anyone had for waiting and, apart from not feeling very confident about the job prospect, nor could I! The work would have been mostly administrative, in fact.

As I was returning to an honorary, missionary-post, I had to set about praying for my air-fare, financial and prayer-partner support, and this all took another couple of months. One ex-Bible college friend was led, most generously, to send me £300 which paid for a one-way plane ticket from Heathrow to Bujumbura, via Nairobi, Kenya. Other friends gave me money and other gifts, while some promised to pray regularly.

John and I had been corresponding for about three months as he was keen for me to make a stopover in Kenya and give my testimony at a small, charismatic conference he was staging at the Kenya coast in August, followed by a family-holiday there. We discussed modes and dates of travel in our letters, and he asked me to arrive at his home in Nakuru on 10th August 1971 at noon, and then travel with him and his family to the coast on the 12th August for the conference.

By early August I was ready to depart, having given notice to CMS and leaving three days free to buy last-minute necessities, pack, etc. I still had some outstanding business to complete in Brussels, so made my first stop there. I arrived in Nairobi on the morning of 7th August 1971 and went to stay at the Anglican (Church of the Province of Kenya) Guest-House there until it was time to move on to Nakuru on the 10th.

Imagine my horror, during supper on the 8th, when seated at a table with other missionaries, to hear one ask another, "Did you hear the sad news that Jane Fulcher has died?" Shocked, but thinking I must have misheard, I leant forward and asked what had been said. I had neither misheard nor misunderstood. I dropped my pudding-spoon into my dish with dismay, and could eat no more. I felt stunned! Whatever would happen now? And poor John and all those children! Of course, the coast-conference and holiday would now have to be cancelled, and tomorrow I vowed to go to a travel-agent to try to arrange an earlier departure date for Burundi ... except that the borders were now closed and likely to remain this way for at least a couple of weeks. "Oh, dear Lord ...!"

Apparently Jane had been eating an early Sunday evening-meal with the two youngest girls, having left baby Paul (aged exactly ten weeks) outside sleeping in his pram, well protected by a mosquito-net and rain-apron. John, meanwhile, had gone to the evening service at his local Anglican Church with the two older girls. Suddenly, as she was eating, Jane keeled sideways on to the dining-room floor, dying instantly. A house-servant had seen her lying by the tea-trolley, just inside the doorway, but imagined at first that she was playing hide-and-seek with the two small girls, so took no immediate notice. However, nine year old Julia and four year old Louise realised that Mummy must be very ill and, after quite a lot of delay, managed to find the correct telephone number of the Vicarage to call Daddy, Anne (aged eleven), and Susan (aged ten) out of church in order to come home and drive Mummy to the hospital.

When John eventually got home, the first thing he did was to lay hands on Jane and pray for her, but to no avail. She had died as she fell, but he took her quickly to the local hospital anyway.

Now there is absolutely no doubt that the Lord could have resurrected her but it was His time to call her Home to Himself, for reasons best known to Him. Life and death are His prerogative and it is not for us to question His motive in allowing one of His children to die at a seemingly premature age. Jane was, in fact, aged thirty eight.

On hearing this news in the Nairobi guest-house I invited all the missionaries at my table to come into my small bedroom for a time of prayer for the bereaved family, and to ask the Lord's wisdom and guidance for my next step also. I remember praying personally that the Lord would, in due time, raise up a replacement-mother for those children, and a wife for

John but, in the meantime, strengthen and comfort them in their loss.

Then I was called to the telephone in the guest house-office. It was John confirming the awful news, but saying that he had already consulted with the Bishop and other elders, and all felt that I should come to Nakuru as pre-arranged, that no plans should be altered regarding the coast and the conference and, they added, "Perhaps this lady could help a little with the children?"

John invited me to attend Jane's funeral the following Tuesday, 10th August 1971 at noon - the very date and time we had agreed by correspondence that I should in any case arrive at his home in Nakuru! Needless to say, the prospect of attending anyone's funeral was not a happy one and I could not help but wonder where I would now be accommodated, but it seemed petty and selfish even to be thinking about myself. However, I had been in Africa long enough previously to know that it would have been quite out of the question even to lodge in the same house as John and the family, and that one had to avoid 'all appearance of evil'. (I Thess. 5:22)

As I was driven to Nakuru by the missionaries whose table I had shared in the guest-house, who were also attending the funeral as close friends of the family, I asked them for ongoing prayer for sensitivity and wisdom about my time with the family after the funeral.

I remember very little about the funeral, except a sense of helplessness as I looked at this lovely family whose eyes were completely dry! The girls all clutched bunches of white Arum Lilies, culled from their garden, to lay on their mother's grave, each child being beautifully clad in a pretty cotton-dress made by

77

Jane. Baby Paul was crying because he had a wet nappy, but quietened down when John took him in his arms while he testified at Jane's graveside of the Lord's personal victory. I had a peculiar, motherly-instinct to want to hold this baby in my own arms, but why? I did not know John at all well, had known Jane even less, and had only met little Louise as far as the children were concerned.

Standing toward the back of the crowd, I felt emotionally unstable and lonely - the very sentiments one would have expected John and the children would be experiencing. Nevertheless, five people at that funeral were given an independent word of knowledge from the Lord: "That lady will be John's second wife!" Of course, I did not know this at the time, or might have boarded the first plane flying anywhere! Jonah would have had nothing on me! Yet none of these people really knew me well, and at least one had never met or spoken to me at all.

After the funeral the lady-missionaries and I went back into Nakuru town for some lunch, and we were then invited to return to John's house for a time of prayer and fellowship. I found myself praying the same prayer I had prayed in the guest-house, "Lord, please send a replacement mother for these children in Your own way and time." What was I saying? Was this not a tactless, insensitive thing to pray? Was it not too soon? No one seemed to think so, and all echoed a hearty, "Amen!"

We were interrupted by baby Paul crying for his milk, and again I had an inexplicable, maternal-desire to hold him and give him his bottle, but kept quiet and still while allowing another 'aunty' to do so!

9. Joyful Mother (Psalm 113:9)

The time of prayer and fellowship following Jane's funeral came to an end, as people had to travel fairly long distances to return home in some cases, and John had an appointment at the local prison, where he ministered to the capital remand cases.

He had begun a week-long fast several days before Jane had died, and it was for this reason that he experienced such victory when she did. That fast continued throughout the funeral and on until the evening before we left for the coast, giving the girls and me only one full day to pack for all of us, including a small baby.

Friends had taken the four girls swimming after the funeral to divert their attention from the sad event. When they returned, the girls made one beeline for the guest-cottage (where I was being accommodated on my own!), which had been lived in earlier by John's late mother. The Lord had it all worked out - I did not have to abstain from any appearance of evil! When the girls arrived, I was sitting on the end of my bed turning up the hem of a dress I needed to pack for the coast. They chatted to me as if they had always known me, calling me 'Aunty' with ease, and all becoming great friends very quickly. Then Anne, the oldest, aged eleven, drawing herself to her full height, announced, "Well, you'll have to be 'Mummy' in the car when we go to the coast on Thursday!" I gulped and dismissed this prophecy as mere childish prattle!

Later on, as I was walking down the cottage-path to take a stroll in the garden, suddenly I saw a complete stranger approaching me. After exchanging brief greetings and backgrounds, he took one look at me and said, "You will *not* be going to Burundi, but are to remain *here!*" I was astounded.

"Who does he think he is?" I questioned reflexively, quite put out! I supposed that John must have briefed him previously.

He was a Jewish believer called Tony and, just the day before, John had received a letter from him in the UK announcing that he was coming because he felt led of the Lord to attend John's conference. Before John had time to turn round or warn anyone, Tony was literally on the doorstep, having arrived from the airport by taxi.

Much later, I discovered that Julia had breezed into her father's bedroom in the main house the next day and brightly asked him, "Daddy, are you going to marry Aunty?" Somewhat taken aback, he muttered that he didn't know, and asked her to run off and allow him to get dressed.

The girls and I worked like beavers the following day, packing one trunk full of cotton clothing and swimwear for everyone to use at the coast; a second trunk containing bed-linen, towels, etc., and a third filled to the brim with basic foodstuffs, since we were going to self-cater. In addition to all this, we had to pack umpteen nappies, feeding-bottles, thermoses, bottle-brush, sterilising-equipment, etc., for the baby, plus a large plastic bowl in which to bath him. Finally, we had to prepare his pram, which fortunately collapsed and lifted off its frame, enabling it to fit in the boot of the car.

The one thing we forgot to pack was long trousers for John! The girls assured me that he only ever wore shorts at the coast because it was so hot. I was to be teased unmercifully for this omission (much needed garb for conference-meetings) and the fact that single ladies could not be expected to know about men's clothing, which was, after all, very true!

There were seven of us, plus a baby, in the car and we had to travel some three hundred and thirty miles all the way to the coast, but spent the first night at Tsavo Inn - a hotel on the main Nairobi-Mombasa road, roughly half-way to the coast. We had this overnight stop for two reasons: firstly because Paul could not digest milk while in motion, and secondly, in order for John's visitors (and primarily me!) to look around the Tsavo West game-park after lunch. I found that I really was 'Mummy' in the car! Paul sat in a plastic baby-seat in the front of John's Peugeot 404 Estate, strapped between John and me, and he was frequently found on my lap when needing special attention. The girls began to be somewhat clinging, and appeared to have adopted me already! They were also vying for my individual attention, rather understandably. "Help, Lord!" was my frequent, silent arrow-prayer!

Somewhat disconcertingly at the hotel reception-desk while John was booking us all in, Anne said to me, "I think you will be sharing a room with Daddy!" I certainly hoped this was only further childlike innocence and, of course, it was! John, Tony and baby Paul shared one room, the girls another, and I a third.

We had an interesting afternoon in the game-park looking at elephant and various other kinds of game. This was the first time I had ever had the opportunity of being in a game-park, despite nearly six years in Africa, so I was quite excited, but aware of my sudden and unexpected responsibilities of being 'Mummy'. There were parts of the game-park where one could get out of the car and proceed on foot, such as Mzima Springs. Somehow I always seemed to be carrying Paul and was becoming increasingly irritated with myself for feeling happily maternal! What had become of this austere career-woman in the past few days?

After the children had eaten their supper and been put to bed, Tony, John and I, with Paul (somehow being carried by me yet again), made our way to the hotel dining-room for supper. It was a chilly, blowy August evening, and I had come to the table wearing a sleeveless dress. I was absolutely frozen, and was just about to excuse myself while I went to my bedroom to collect a cardigan when John offered me his unwanted Tweed jacket! It was a chivalrous and charming gesture I would not be allowed to forget in a hurry. I was not used to having protective men around!

On the way to the coast the next morning, John apologised that he had quite forgotten to tell me that he was due to collect a lady-visitor from South Africa the following day, whom the Lord had saved through John's ministry in the sixties while both were on UK leave, and she now wanted to attend his conference. He also went on to explain that we would stop in Mombasa for lunch, where he would have to spend time alone writing to his parents-in-law to share fuller details of their daughter's death and funeral, as he had only managed to send them a brief word on this matter.

It was just as well that we did not have to collect Mary from her plane from South Africa that same day or it really would have been a squash, especially with yet more luggage! Even now we could have done greater justice to a mini-bus than a Peugeot Estate, if not a double-decker! But there most definitely would not be 'any appearance of evil' once Mary arrived, for John had his escort in Tony and I had mine in Mary! The Lord had made every provision, especially as we were all to live under one roof at the coast.

It was late afternoon by the time the family, Tony and I had arrived at the conference-centre and had moved into the bungalow we were renting on the same compound, bordering the Indian Ocean. Mary and I were destined to share one of the three available bedrooms, while Tony and the rest followed the same sleeping-accommodation pattern as at the hotel en-route.

Basically I found myself responsible for Paul, housekeeping and shopping-lists, although John had sent on ahead a couple of his workers to help. "Horrors!" I reflected, "I've got to be 'Mummy' to this entire house-party of nine people, not just the children themselves!"

The conference began next evening, and the programme was planned to include morning and evening sessions with afternoons free for personal rest, fellowship and swimming, etc. I am always grateful when conferences are not crammed with all-day sessions, breaking only briefly for meals. I simply end up exhausted, with spiritual indigestion, and cannot remember who said what. John proved to be of like-mind.

Incredible though this may seem, and quite out of character with both John and me, the Lord had spoken very clearly during the week of conference-meetings at the coast that I was not to fly on to Burundi at all, which Tony himself had first told me by word of knowledge on the evening of the funeral, at which he himself was not present.

I have to confess to being a little naïve when the Lord first spoke direct to me prophetically, saying, "You will not proceed to Burundi but remain here to care for these children."

"But Lord," I argued, proud and incredulous, "I am not called to be a *nursemaid*, and … I thought *You* had told me from Your Word that I had been called to a land of hills and valleys (Deut. 11:11), and … also that I was to 'get me up this way southward, and go up into the mountain' (Num. 13:17), and also Lord, You know that I have now qualified as a teacher-of-typewriting. What has staying here, looking after children, got to do with all that?"

It did not occur to me that I was not simply being called to be a nursemaid but also to become the very replacement-wife and mother for whom I myself had personally been inspired to pray!! Clearly one needs to beware how one prays, but I believe that, in retrospect, I was being led by the Lord to pray prophetically and answer my own prayer. In one short week it had become lucid. The Lord was actually asking me to *marry* John and become the mother of his ready-made family. I hoped He was telling John the same thing which, of course, He was!

Kenya is also a land of hills and valleys and is South East of Britain. Nakuru itself is some 6,000 feet above sea-level and just as 'mountainous' in altitude as much of Burundi. But I had a deep love for Burundi, and had very mixed feelings about not returning there.

Obviously the Lord was not asking either of us to marry out of *cold* obedience. A close affection had begun to grow between us, but we were afraid it was all too soon. But by whose standards? We had been brought up to 'respect the dead', but the girls were already starting to look to me as their replacement-mother. With some trepidation we shared our guidance with the Pentecostal minister who had come to speak at the conference. He smiled broadly and said, "Yes, I know dears! You see, the Lord told me by word of knowledge on the day of the funeral!" We were flabbergasted! He and I had not so much as exchanged words at the funeral, but he and his wife were at John's house for the prayer-meeting afterwards and had heard my prayer *after* the Lord had already let him into the secret, and now he was beginning to see the fulfilment! He was delighted. However, others were *not*, which is understandable.

On the last night of the conference it was felt that I should not only give my testimony but add the bombshell about our eventual marriage. Frankly, I dreaded that part, as I could imagine how some folk would be bound to react this soon after Jane's death, even if at this stage it was simply to announce our forthcoming engagement. I chickened out somewhat, in that I testified so far and then asked John to take over!

One expatriate-lady immediately rose to her feet in a huff, scraping her chair noisily on the floor, and stalked out in disgust. She had come from Nakuru with her husband and family and had felt particularly close to Jane. She was, by nature, very hot-headed and reactionary, yet I sympathised. We too would normally have felt it was all too speedy and that it would be prudent to wait a year and see how the Lord led. Yet what was the point in waiting? We did not have to save up to buy and furnish a home - in fact, we now had the contents of three homes to combine - John's, his late mother's, and mine. We might possibly even have to get rid of some things!

While this lady and her family returned to Nakuru and she got busy spreading the news of our future engagement all around the expatriate-population of the town, with her own interpretations and embellishments, we remained on at the coast, all nine of us, for some holiday.

I had to spend quite a lot of my time inside the house writing to those who were expecting me in Burundi, plus prayer-partners, informing them that I would not be going to Burundi and why. I had to tackle a lot of correspondence and make many fresh arrangements.

One amusing thing that happened is that, when I had originally arrived in Nairobi, I had purchased a railway ticket to enable me to travel back from Mombasa to Nairobi by train in order to catch my onward flight to Burundi, ostensibly leaving John and the family holidaying at the coast. When John and I now examined that train ticket, in order to obtain a refund on it, what should it read but Nairobi-Mombasa instead of Mombasa-Nairobi, so it would have been quite useless anyway as it stood, and these things are not very simple or quick to have altered in Africa! Quite unlike me, I had bought the ticket in a hurry and not checked it to discover that it enabled me only to travel in the reverse direction! It was yet another confirmation I was never meant to travel anywhere away from John and the children.

Another confirmation was from a missionary working in Kenya who, like me, was a commercial teacher. She had invited me to visit her college while I was in the country, if time permitted, so I had also to write and explain to her why I could not come at that time, saying that I felt intrinsically bound up with this family. To my surprise, she replied that I should at all costs obey the Lord, and assured me of her blessing.

Suddenly too, I remembered my peculiar, one-off shopping list-prayer in Twickenham, tabulating what turned out to be a precise description of John himself! He ticked all the right boxes, plus!

The ultimate and most important confirmation came from God's own Word in Psalm 113:9, 'He maketh the barren woman to keep house, and to be a *joyful mother* of children. Praise ye the Lord'! We *all* praised Him, indeed!

During the coast holiday, the children had begun to call me 'Mummy', yet it did not feel in the least bit strange to any of us, but perfectly natural. The children had clamoured all along for us to, "hurry up and get on with it." The only thing that was not natural to them was that, for some reason they could not understand, Mummy slept in a different bedroom from Daddy and continued to do so up to the time they were married!

There was no opportunity during, or immediately after, the holiday to purchase an engagement ring and, in fact, on arriving back in Nakuru in the evening, a young man was waiting on John's doorstep for urgent counsel. John invited me to join in the ministry and it seemed a further seal upon our relationship, not only to marry, but to minister together to others in need. We did so in perfect tandem.

We were very tired after the long journey. The children were able to go ahead and bath and eat, but we had to put the Lord's work first (with the exception of changing Paul's nappy and giving him his feed, of course), and we have endeavoured to make this a principle in our lives ever since. The man who had come for prayer left rejoicing, healed in body, mind and spirit, for which we gave all the glory to our Great Physician.

Each evening, after supper, we had a short time of reading God's Word and prayer with all the children. I then wended my weary way across to the guest-cottage, but suddenly felt bereft and curiously alone after living in a community of nine people for the past couple of weeks at the coast! I had such a sense of loss and loneliness that it was difficult even to apply myself with full concentration on essentials.

Mary had since returned to South Africa and we had dropped Tony off in Naivasha on the way back from the coast to stay with our Pentecostal minister-friend in order to take on any spiritual engagements that opened up to him. Tony had spoken at a number of the conference meetings and led the worship, with the help of his autoharp, but in fact very little other ministry came his way. It seemed that the Lord's sole purpose in bringing him was simply to deliver God's Word to me and be an escort for John. He returned to stay with John again, but left for England before we were married, saying (this time *not* by word of knowledge) that he hoped we would have twins of our own!

During Tony's return-visit to Nakuru, John invited him to join us all on a family-outing to Lake Nakuru, with its surrounding game-park. Tony was, of course, delighted at the prospect, and all eight of us piled into the car with a tea-picnic.

John stopped the car on a particular road in the game park to point out waterbuck, when one of the girls asked John, "Daddy, could we go for a 'whee'?" (which she pronounced 'wee'). Immediately Tony began to look out of the car windows on all sides but, look as he may, he saw not a single bush or tree in sight, but only a murram road with short blades of grass on either side at that specific spot. He had, of course, interpreted the request as one requiring a 'bush loo', and began to go hot and cold at the prospect of all female passengers descending right there and then, in full view not only of himself but any other passers-by!! What the girls were actually wanting was for John to drive at speed on the next stretch of the same road where there was a ramp ahead, causing a sensation of 'flying' over the top, when all the children would chorus, "Whee!"

John, realising that Tony had suddenly become uncharacteristically quiet and that he was busily looking all around for non-existent bushes, or even a cement-block building duly marked 'WC', explained what the girls really meant. This led to so many giggles and red faces that it took John some minutes to regain total equilibrium, before re-accelerating along the imaginary runway! It is, in any case, forbidden just to get out of one's car unless at a recognised picnic-site or viewpoint, marked by a signpost to that effect, but, even then, one alights at one's own risk.

The other childish delight at Lake Nakuru was to get the car-tyres stuck in the muddy, receding lake-shore, and be forced to empty the car of passengers, who then competed as to who could get the muddiest in putting rubber mats and bunches of grass or reeds under the offending tyres and push to enable John to drive us on to firmer ground!

It is always difficult to persuade children born and bred in Africa to wear any form of footwear, apart from flip-flops. Invariably, ours would return from lake-trips caked in mud up to their knees!

A regular feature when visiting the lake was for all the children to sit on the car roof-rack in safe areas while John or I drove along relatively slowly, but we had to take care in windy conditions which caused soda-dust to blow in their eyes. This dust proves highly allergenic to many people, making eyes and throat exceedingly sore, and Lake Nakuru is even capable of

89

blowing its soda-deposits for a long distance in dry-season winds. I had personally to avoid trips to soda-lakes, wherever possible, in this kind of weather.

As soon as we had a free day, before the older children were due to resume boarding-school, we all went to Nairobi to buy an engagement-ring. Imagine the Asian jeweller's odd expression when, one after another, the girls were saying to me, "But Mummy, this ring is much nicer, isn't it Daddy?" and "Mummy, try this one" or "Oh please, Daddy, buy this one for Mummy. It's so pretty and looks lovely on her finger!"

The man's eyes got wider and wider. It was written all over his puzzled face, "Why have they waited all these years, until they have five children, to bother to get engaged?"

Having at last chosen a beautiful dark blue, oval sapphire surrounded by tiny diamonds, John then asked the jeweller about gold wedding-rings. This was almost too much for the jeweller! But custom is custom, and who was he to argue! I had told John that I hoped especially that we might exchange identical gold-bands and have inscribed on the inside of each Psalm 34:3 - "O magnify the Lord with me, and let us exalt His name together!" He thought this a splendid idea and arranged for one of his late father's gold tie-pins to be melted down and made into a ring to match the one he had purchased for me, and to have both inscribed.

The only engagement-party we had was the seven of us in the jeweller's shop, with Paul's pram in tow, all happily admiring the sapphire ring now placed by John on the third finger of my left hand, with our faces all aglow! That was the only celebration we needed and it seemed to provide plenty of entertainment for the jeweller as well! After all, it wasn't every day that couples with several children went into his shop to buy engagement *and* wedding-rings, but these Europeans are such an unknown quantity! And what an enigma it must have been that we were so much in love after having that brood!

John had pre-planned to go on a prisons mission early in October and felt that we should marry before then, as that would delay things and make it very hard for us *outwardly* to continue being 'Mummy and Daddy', 'husband and wife' by day, and yet otherwise live independent lives. We came to the conclusion, therefore, that 25th September 1971 was to be *the* great day, with the four girls acting as bridesmaids.

Our Pentecostal minister-friend agreed to marry us in John's local Anglican church, because the then vicar and his wife did not approve of John remarrying so soon and they had counselled that, instead, Louise, Paul and I should all go to a farm some thirty miles distant and remain there for three months as a sign of respect for the dead, and to test our love for each other.

While they had a point, we could not agree to this as it would have deprived Louise and Paul of their one remaining blood-parent, and John would have been left entirely comfortless, splitting, as it would have done, the whole family and disrupting Louise's home- and nursery-school life. None of us could take that kind of responsibility and its consequences, least of all the children.

Yet was 25th September *too* soon? Humanly speaking it was, being only seven short weeks since Jane had died. However, we knew it was not quick in the Lord's reckoning of time, a day being as a thousand years in His sight (2 Peter 3:8), and that Jane would never have wanted her husband or children neglected, particularly her baby son. And we dared not ignore the prophecies He had given to me, with confirmation and fulfilment! To say nothing of my own prophetic prayer in Twickenham.

10. And the Wedding was Furnished with Guests (Matt. 22:10b)

John had taken to introducing me light-heartedly to his expatriate Christian friends as "his unmarried Mum"! It can be imagined how I viewed this, however true it was in *one* sense. And fortunately none of them misconstrued his meaning.

There was much to do between our engagement and our wedding, with under a month in which to complete everything, including preparing the three older girls to return to boarding-school at St Andrew's Preparatory School, Turi, some thirty miles away.

Each boarder had a huge metal trunk which had to come home at the end of every term for checking contents, repairing and replenishing, where necessary, all essential uniform, games-kit, etc. The only way to get through all this in the time was to call out one item at a time from the clothing-list, with each child standing in front of her opened trunk at one end of the sitting-room, and rummaging to find the appropriate object. We then examined this together and decided whether it needed buttons, patches or darning, or if it should be passed on to the next youngest sister or consigned to the rag-bag. I must have sounded like a sergeant-major doing roll-call! What a relief it was to us all when that job was completed - not only then, but in all the ensuing school-holidays! Obviously I taught the girls to sew by hand whatever was within their scope.

We had purchased white bridal, and blue bridesmaids' dress-materials when we had gone to Nairobi to get my engagement-ring, and a Goan tailor in Nakuru was busily stitching our regalia to meet the deadline. Goan tailors in Kenya in that era were amazingly clever and could make up a dress simply by copying from a picture of the style required. I had also managed to buy a veil in Nairobi on the same occasion, plus white shoes for 'all of us gals'.

Then there was a decision to be made about our order-of-marriage service, the choosing of hymns and going through a mock ceremony to make sure we all knew what to do and when. The minister's wife suggested that it would be different, and rather lovely, if each of the girls was to walk behind me in single-file as I entered the church, with Anne bringing up the rear as my chief-bridesmaid. She was to take charge of my white Bible with a floral-spray on its satin-bookmark during the repeating of the vows. Invitations also has to be printed and sent out, and arrangements made with caterers, as I had more than I could handle just then to undertake the cooking and preparation of a buffet-breakfast for at least fifty people.

As I was no longer able to return to Burundi, John and I felt it would be very fitting, and a tremendous privilege for us, if one of the co-founders of the then Ruanda Mission, Dr Algie Stanley Smith and his wife, Zoë, could act as my 'parents'. They were on leave that summer in England seeing various members of their family but, by a God-incidence, managed to combine attending our wedding in Kenya on their way back to Uganda after visiting their daughter in Nigeria.

The 'Algies' (as they were affectionately called in Mission-circles) stayed in our guest-cottage for a few days after the wedding (officially vacated by me at last, much to the relief of the children!) with another very distinguished guest - Miss Mary Sharp, a CMS missionary and the daughter of the other co-

94

founder of the Ruanda Mission, Dr Leonard Sharp. It was impossible to have better Mission-representation.

Interestingly enough, Mary Sharp had been in on our relationship right from the beginning. When we went to the coast-conference, she and her father had their home on the Kikambala Conference Centre site, not far from Mombasa, where John's conference had been held, and she fellowshipped with us privately and in many of the meetings. She believed the arrangement made by John in correspondence with me to arrive at his house on what turned out to be the very date and time of Jane's funeral, was prophetically significant.

The morning of our wedding-day found the four girls (the three oldest ones home from boarding-school for the occasion) and me, sitting at the local Scottish hairdressers having our hair shampooed and set. Before leaving the main-house I had left an exceedingly large beef-and-vegetable stew simmering in preparation for thirteen people to sit down to lunch, including ourselves.

After lunch, I went back to the guest-cottage for the last time to have a leisurely bath prior to dressing in my finery! Just before it was time to leave for the church, the heavens opened and torrents of rain fell from the skies, but the Africans always look upon rain as a sign of blessing. Meanwhile, I was wondering how I was going to be able to walk to the car, parked outside the main-house, over exceedingly wet grass, with a full-length white dress and court-shoes! I need not have worried, for John himself drove right up to the cottage-door and, because Christians are not superstitious, lifted my veil and kissed me! He then helped me into the waiting-car, draped with old, clean sheets to keep our wedding-garments unspotted. I had to

95

wonder how many brides were driven to church by their prospective husbands, but John would hear of no one else chauffeuring his bride in case she changed her mind!

The girls, magnificently dressed in identical long, blue dresses with fresh freesias wired to headbands decorating their hair, and carrying, like me, white Bibles with matching flowers attached to satin-bookmarks, had gone ahead in another car and were waiting for me outside the church. Mercifully, by now the sun was shining once more.

It had been agreed that taped music would accompany me as I walked down the aisle on 'Dad's' arm, but the friend responsible for switching on the tape-recorder quite forgot, and we walked down in majestic silence which the congregation found even more moving, in fact, than any musical-accompaniment! I had had such a domesticated morning and so played the part of 'wife and mother' that, when it came actually to walking down the aisle, I did so as if I were going shopping! I was amazed at my lack of usual nervousness. John had been standing at the front of the church waiting for some time but, with the forgotten music, there had been a delay in cueing us to process, and he began to think I *had* changed my mind and thumbed a lift back home!

The service was so beautiful and moving that the African guests, in particular, wished they could go through their own marriage-ceremonies all over again! A missionary-family from Nairobi attended our wedding and their smallest daughter, when at another missionaries' wedding (single lady to widower), asked her mother, "But Mummy, where is the baby?"

The reception was held in our large garden. We had ordered a three-tiered, iced wedding-cake, but the icing on the

96

second-tier had failed to set hard, and the pillars holding the top-tier began to sink into its neighbour below! We had to be content with just two, but it was just as well, as the children of one of our workers broke into the dining-room and scoffed almost a whole tier and, besides feeding all the guests, there were relatives and friends in England to whom we wanted to post portions.

I found it rather sad to be deprived of a taste of our own wedding-cake on our wedding-day because of the greed and indiscipline of those children, but we had to forgive. We have found it typical again and again since that day in different circumstances but, equally typically, we have to be gracious and forgiving, yet challenging the culprit, where appropriate, in a spirit of prayerfulness, meekness and love. One has to remember that Africans rarely eat sweet things and so cakes are a real luxury to them. And they are not used to tiny morsels, but consume whole platefuls at a sitting!

We were unable to take a honeymoon at once because of John's pre-planned mission to the Naivasha Prison. In order not to be absent from us so soon after our marriage, he installed Paul, Louise and me in a Naivasha hotel and took his meals there so that we would see him for an hour or two each day. Nevertheless, the time tended to drag, and boredom and loneliness set in for Louise and me and, with hindsight, it might have been better to remain at home for those four days so that Louise could have continued with nursery-school, and where the children had their playthings readily to hand and I had much to occupy my time.

In November we booked a beach-cottage on the North Coast near Malindi and had three lovely weeks' honeymoon-proper, with Louise and Paul accompanying us. Paul was, by this time, five and a half months' old and thoroughly enjoyed being dipped in the sea. One day, John, who enjoyed the water, announced that he was going to take Louise and me for a little sail. Imagine our disbelief when he hired something so small that Louise and I dubbed it 'a bread-board with a teacloth-sail'! It *was* a 'little sail' indeed! We hung on for dear life, both being non-swimmers at that time, and John could see that neither of us was actually enjoying this water-sport, so offered to drop us off down the beach. Louise, at the age of nearly four and three quarters, was so funny. As we touched dry land, she looked up at me and said. "Phew! What a relief!", and we burst into laughter as we walked hand-in-hand up to our rented cottage higher up the beach, leaving John to return the 'bread-board' to the hotel from which he had hired it, and walk back.

We became quite concerned during that honeymoon because I was having tremendous nausea and all the outward symptoms of pregnancy, which was certainly not planned and could not, theoretically, be the case. In fact, it wasn't at all, and on referring this to a New Zealand minister who came to stay with us on our return, he replied, "Well, of course, it makes sense!"

"Whatever do you mean?" we chorused, thinking he suspected something untoward.

"No, no!" he reassured us, "I know you weren't pregnant, but you see other people in Nakuru decided you *were*, and rumour-mongered that you had had to have a 'shotgun-wedding'. Therefore, the power of their words produced symptoms of pregnancy."

This was new teaching to us, and it took us time to assimilate and believe it and, above all, test it against the scriptures. Our policy has always been, "If in doubt, sling it out," particularly if it does not line up with God's Word. However, when we fasted and prayed, and verbally forgave each guilty person individually (all of whom were European Christians, including missionaries, and especially women), praying in the name of Jesus and by the power of His name, all nausea and symptoms disappeared at once and never returned. The Lord also confirmed it through Proverbs 18:20,21.

We have met similar situations in others again and again. The tongue is a very powerful instrument for good or evil, as the book of James teaches. Verbalised, negative and even untrue statements have marked effects either on the subject, the object, or both. A ministry of deliverance is always needed to cut that person off from their effects through the all-powerful name of Jesus.

We maintained a daily morning Quiet Time. On waking, we would read our Bibles and pray individually - in my case, while I was bottle-feeding Paul, sitting up in bed. Then after lunch from around 2 p.m. until 4 p.m., while Paul had his nap or played near us in the garden in his play-pen, we had joint-times of prayer and intercession. We would often fast one day per week, omitting breakfast and lunch, and taking only water. Sometimes this may extend to two or three days, causing me a big spiritual battle with physical weakness, dizziness and weight-loss on Day 2! But there is nothing novel in that particular attack of the evil one. And he was the more defeated as the Lord began to add new gifts of the Holy Spirit, which I had not specifically asked for, nor instantly recognised. Nevertheless, like a number of charismatics in their early experiences of the gifts, we became far too insular, praying mainly together, and on one occasion had a subjective vision that proved devastating. Out of this difficult experience we learnt to be extremely careful, and weigh everything first against the scriptures and, if appropriate, wait for quite independent, uninformed witnesses by way of added confirmation. We realised that if one wanted something of personal benefit, even if it involved other people, it was possible to receive subjective guidance or even directly satanic guidance to lead one astray. But it was during such times of prayer, and while I was in England following my time in Burundi, that the beginnings of a prophetic ministry were established, although I was blissfully unaware of it then!

A few months after our marriage, in the New Year of 1972, it was necessary for me to go into hospital for a very minor operation. European tongues were still wagging, and so it was of great sadness to realise that a key-person in leadership was the instigator of the terrible lie that I had gone in to have an abortion. This implied I must either have been pregnant out of wedlock or immediately afterwards. It was not *we* who were affected this time but, strangely enough, my ex-arch enemy, who had marched out at the coast-conference when our forthcoming engagement was announced. This time she was to stand as my arch-defender! She rounded on her prey like a female cat facing feline competition, claws out and fur flying, saying to the person in question, "How *dare* you? She would *never* contemplate abortion at any price. She has gone into hospital to have quite a different operation, and it is none of your business anyway!" This was enough to silence any gossip, and her words (plus our prayers, and doubtless her own, together with our earlier forgivenesses) were even more powerful and effective than all the backbiting!

We continued blessing by name all the gossips and persecutors, and one-by-one they changed, without their knowing why, and began inviting us round to their homes and being open and friendly once again! One such lady gave us a magnificent framed- tapestry of Jesus handing Peter the keys of the kingdom, and she told us most graciously that it was a belated wedding-gift. We were deeply touched and grateful. It was, perhaps, symbolic that she, as if representing the rest of the anti-brigade of earlier days, was handing us the keys of release and welcome, because this event was a breakthrough. God is our Vindicator and Victor! Hallelujah!

11. No Continuing City (Hebrews 13:14)

John had been renting his bungalow in Nakuru for several years, with its guest-cottage, set in five acres of gardens with rolling lawns, flowers and shrubs, including a circular rose-garden at the front. Out of the blue, we were advised that the property had been put on the market and sold! A local Asian businessman, hearing via the usual bush-telegraph, before we did, that it was up for sale, flew immediately to England, contacted the owner, paid cash on the nail, and we were given notice to quit!

We were quite desolate, as John had himself contemplated purchasing earlier but decided against it. This time we were not even offered a second chance or informed that it was up for sale! Unfurnished, large family-sized properties were not easy to come by in Nakuru in June 1972, but eventually we found a slightly dilapidated farmhouse to rent with seventeen large rooms, and a separate six-roomed guest-cottage, built on a two-acre plot a few miles outside Nakuru, between Lanet and Mbaruk.

What a hassle it was to pack up! There were John's late mother's possessions and furniture in the guest-cottage; my things which had arrived from the UK, plus all his own belongings and yet more furniture in the main-house. It took weeks to get it all contained in boxes, crates, trunks and oil-drums, etc., and, as we got nearer to moving-date in the August, John and I had to get up every day at 3 a.m., while Paul was still asleep, to finish the last-minute packing. It was a relief on

Sundays to be able to sleep on until Paul woke at 05.45 for his breakfast.

Paul had begun walking during this time. He had taken to standing behind an old wooden-horse on wheels, which had been passed down through the entire family. We would take it and him out in the garden and, standing at the bottom of the steps leading to our front-door, he would hold on to the handle behind the horse, with a daring grin all over his face, and waddle faster and faster like a duck as he pushed 'Neddy' down the gently-sloping grass, until finally he fell over in a giggling heap, leaving Neddy careering ahead, unmanned!

Inside the house, he would grope around furniture and his playpen, until one triumphant day he took off unaided, shouting, "Ook, Mummy, I 'awkin'!" For some strange reason he chose to omit most initial consonants when he began both to walk and talk!

As a baby, Paul had an abhorrence of all orange-coloured food, such as carrots, paw-paw, oranges, etc. No matter how one would disguise these and mix them with other stronger-flavoured and darker-coloured food, he would *always* detect and vomit up the whole lot! I had to buy an enormous plastic-tablecloth to put under his high-chair against this eventuality, or the rug would have been ruined. It was a peculiar phenomenon, because he came to like all of these foods a little later. Also, from the age of seven, he was asking for an 'orange bedroom', it suddenly becoming his number-one colour!

Paul's favourite bittersweet story-book, which I asked to read to him every day from around the age of two, was 'The Ugly Duckling'. Whenever we reached the sad-part, he would turn over several pages, with tears in his eyes, asking me

103

not to read 'that bit', and recognising from the pictures in the book where the safety-zones were! Provided those were adhered to, he would listen quite happily every day, with a measure of addiction.

Moving was a mixed blessing, as we discovered the new house was haunted, and this was confirmed by a number of other friends. We could not determine its exact history, but rumour had it that an Irish wake had been held there when the previous farmer-owner had died. We also heard that his widow had decided to make her thirteen year-old son a replacement ballroom-dancing partner, treating him more like a gigolo than a son, but certainly the property needed exorcising.

We had some ornamental Arab copper-trays in two back-to-back open fireplaces in the hall and sitting-room and, every now and then, despite a lack of wind, they would rattle and trill. Cupboards would groan and creak, and on one occasion I was lying in bed when suddenly a white-apparition passed in front of our bed, and I was most definitely *not* dreaming, for I had only just put out the light and begun to settle down. I was terrified, and my screams brought John hotfoot from the sitting-room to pray for me. It took some time, nevertheless, for me to be calmed and regain my equilibrium sufficiently to fall asleep.

Early in 1973 the three youngest children were home for the Christmas-New Year holidays and had seen two tiny kittens with their mother huddled in one corner of an empty outhouse. "Oh please, Mummy, please, let us have one, just one!" they pleaded. I did not need much persuading, being the cat-lover I am, so we agreed that once the kittens were about six weeks old we would go and choose the one we wanted.

By this time our garden-helper had taken the mother-cat and two kittens into his own house, intent on keeping one of the twin kittens. When we entered the house, the choice was a foregone conclusion. There was one tiny coal-black kitten, who spat and hissed at us with his back arched and fur standing on end, from the far wall of the one-roomed house. The moment we approached it behaved more like a spitting cobra than a cat! By complete contrast, the other was mainly white, with creamy markings on her back and having distinct Siamese features mixed with Persian soft, long, fluffy hair. Added to that was some 'Heinz 57' producing a typical chocolate-brown tail, black paw-patches and ears, and tear-marks either side of her nose! She closely resembled her mother, who had clearly come from Siamese stock, but this kitten was much prettier, with striking blue eyes. She was affectionate and gentle, and didn't mind one scrap when the children stroked and fondled her.

We carried her home as if she were a prized piece of Dresden China, and rummaged in the pantry for a small carton which we lined with some old, clean rags to make her a bed. I had to sacrifice one of my roasting-tins to make a litter-tray, but had many willing hands to meet the needs of this ball of fluff. "What shall we call her?" I asked the children. We all thought hard. "Well, take a good look at her fur," I suggested. "What does it remind you of?"

"Smoke!" said Julia.

"Yes, I know, Smokey!" offered Louise.

"es, 'mokey!" agreed Paul, with a protective pat. So, that important detail settled, Smokey became one of the family and was deeply loved and treasured.

Being part-Siamese, she had, on occasions, a true Siamese yowl. Particularly when the girls were home for the holidays, Smokey would sit on the mat by the French- doors in the front-hall and yowl to see who would call out or come running to collect her first. This caused a great deal of competition among the oldest girls, whose bedrooms were all adjacent down a corridor leading off the front-hall, whereas Louise and Paul were ensconced in adjoining-rooms at the opposite end of the house in what was rather grandly labelled by our landlord, 'the parental suite' containing two internal-verandahs, our vast bedroom, dressing-room and en-suite bathroom, with small fry in single rooms next door.

We went for evening walks most days, when Louise and Paul would ride tricycles (and later bicycles) along the straight, but bumpy, dirt farm-track. Smokey would accompany us the full length of our long garden drive and sit on a fence post awaiting our return. She never felt safe to venture off the plot itself. If anyone was sitting in the garden to pray or play, she would gallop up to them, either to sit by them or on their laps. Louise and Paul developed the habit of lying on their tummies to read, and invariably Smokey would be found sitting like a broody hen in the middle of one of their backs!

She was a marvellous ratter, and would go up into the rafters and bring down her trophies for all to admire. She would drop the rat from her mouth just long enough to give a very loud yowl to attract everyone's attention and, having got an audience, would proceed to throw the rat into the air, prance ballerina-style on her back-legs while giving the rat a left-hook, and then let it crash to the ground once more with a dull thud. She would feign lack of interest by looking around her while sitting near her prey but, if it twitched one whisker, she would paw it, daring it to escape. Finally, when she was assured it really was dead, she would crunch it up and then yowl at the top of her voice and chirrup for a large saucer of milk to quench her thirst!

Once we had acquired a rather ferocious Alsatian guard-dog, Smokey virtually lived on the corrugated roof-sheets because she had every right to fear him, but he was, of course, a magnificent watchman. We would have to tie Amigo up while we coaxed Smokey down with food and then shut her in an indoor-store overnight, leaving her bed, litter-tray and victuals in there with her. In fact, she was a deterrent to any rats who sought refuge in the store, or in the house as a whole.

Within a year of moving to this haunted house, bad health began to manifest itself in some members of the family. Paul had a couple of rather frightening asthmatic turns at night as a toddler, when John and I had to go into his bedroom and play at lighting and blowing out candles or inflating paper bags in order to restore his normal breathing-pattern. Then he had a chest-infection that lasted for two and a half months, causing fevers, nausea and dehydration to an alarming extent whereby he could not digest even sips of water, let alone keep down antibiotics. Finally, he had a very nasty bout of Sinusitis with Bronchitis, keeping us awake at nights. We took him to a Nairobi based charismatic meeting where the Lord miraculously healed him as a result of prayer, with the laying-on of hands. His nose began to run so much thereafter that we got through a box of tissues in no time! As one American lady-missionary put it, "The Lord sure unplugged him!" What a sense of rejoicing and relief we had!

107

Anne also began fresh symptoms, at the age of twelve, of the Petit-Mal she had had for a few months when she was six, and she now began walking into things and having disturbing trances. She had to take large capsules for a time but, quite independent of us, she sought spiritual-healing while at a charismatic conference and decided to stop taking medication immediately! We did not discover this until five days later, but there was no doubt, the Lord had very definitely healed her and she has never had any recurrence, for which we praise His Name!

Then I went down with Mucous Colitis, which became worse and worse over a four-year period, until my weight was down to just over seven stone and I was so weak that I could barely walk. In the end I had to be treated in the Nairobi Hospital.

At first we did not see the connection between the sickness and the house, but called monthly days of prayer and fasting, and eventually asked a particular Kenyan Evangelist to cleanse the house by prayer, which he did unsuccessfully. Years later we discovered that this man was a total hypocrite, who had taken on two extra wives and was sleeping around with prostitutes and drinking home-brewed gin, called *chang'aa*.

Although each of us was totally healed, we are not really convinced that that house has ever been successfully exorcised to this day. Our daughter Julia has visited it once or twice since as an adult, and felt strangely faint while there each time. She is not at all prone to passing out, nor was she consciously thinking about it or the fact that the house had been haunted, and she certainly was not unwell prior to her visits. John was to begin manifesting sickness later on also.

In the mid-seventies, all seven of us were attending a large, charismatic conference in Nairobi when our Peugeot 404, seven-seater car was permanently stolen. The car had been parked in a public car-park which was directly overlooked by Police HQ! This was a tremendous challenge to our faith, as we only ever had minimum compulsory insurance-cover. Such thefts were very common, many cars having their number-plates changed by their new 'owners' before driving the vehicles over one or other of the borders into neighbouring-countries, and/or being used for spare parts. Peugeot 404s were popular as seven-seater taxis.

Mercifully, we had a Peugeot 304 Estate at home, which we had shipped back to Kenya after our 1973 UK leave, so John was able to go back to Nakuru by taxi and return in the 304 to Nairobi. This car was not nearly so roomy for seven people, plus luggage, but we had all crowded into it in the UK, and my parents had had two special, folding, deep foam-cushions made to put either side of the boot, so that Louise and Paul could travel as 'baggage'.

After the loss of our Peugeot 404, John was forced to take the one remaining 304 on Sundays to Nakuru Prison where he continued to hold services for the capital-remand cases, and rarely got back home until the afternoon. This meant that Sunday School had to take place mostly in the home during school holidays, if I was unable to get a lift to church. Unfortunately, morning service at church did not coincide with John's arrival at the prison but, even if it had, I should still have had to try to get a lift home again. Only one couple passed our door who attended the same church, and they did not worship regularly in the mornings as they were resident-teachers at a nearby boarding-school.

The children were all, generally speaking, very easy to bring up, being well-mannered and disciplined and very open and responsive. However, as is often the case, changes began to be seen in some of them as they prepared to take 'O'-levels, which is a very tense time for young people, when one is neither child nor adult.

12. Lovers of Hospitality? (Titus 1:6-9)

One of the biggest difficulties in sending one's children overseas to boarding-school is finding and appointing guardians. In our case, we had no suitable relatives who could take on this task and, in any case, none was Christian.

At first, a couple who had been in Kenya earlier and had been friends of John and Jane, offered to become guardians around the time of Jane's death, before they knew of my existence. The husband had become ordained since returning to the UK, so we prayed at length and trusted that their guardianship would work well.

They were exceedingly kind to our first two girls, who started UK boarding-school at the same time in September 1973, which had deliberately coincided with our first UK leave. However, when John and I were invited to go to this couple's home with all the children in tow, because their house sported no less than eight bedrooms, we realised that they were unable to accept me as Jane's replacement, or our marriage, and it was not long before we saw that their guardianship would not work as far as we personally were concerned.

They had perhaps responded sentimentally at first, for obvious and understandable reasons, but in practice were critical and condemning of John. In fact, during our weekend visit to their home, we went to their church and the husband-minister was so ill-at-ease that he was unable to preach his sermon without distraction. We realised that this was due to the sad fact that he could neither forgive nor forget.

Another ex-Kenya missionary couple then offered to become guardians, and they were ideal and we all got on extremely well. I was totally accepted and was able to relate with ease to both husband and wife. This husband was also a minister, who later lost his wife and returned to Kenya as a missionary-bishop. Interestingly enough, he himself re-married and his second wife was also a missionary with four children who was widowed the very same year that he was bereaved.

Our friends had four children of their own, and their two girls attended the same boarding-school as ours, so guardianship was comparatively easy and convenient.

By the time they took over the guardianship, our third daughter had joined her sisters at school in Britain, so their guardians might have as many as seven children (ours plus theirs) in their home for half-terms, unless ours visited elsewhere, which they did frequently. For most of the main holidays they flew back to Kenya to us, unless they were preparing for their 'O'-level examinations, which included visiting France in order to become fluent in French, and this was a subject which both Anne and Julia sat and passed well.

When the time came for this lovely couple's own daughters to leave the school, it became impossible for them to continue their guardianship, living as they were, a long way from the school. They had really gone the second-mile and been so loving and understanding toward us all, and we were so sad that the time had now come prayerfully to find replacements.

Eventually, yet another ex-missionary couple offered to become guardians. They had served the Lord in another East African country and, once again, they were a ministerial-couple. The wife was exceptionally strong, ruling not only her own family but seeking to do likewise with ours, and playing one of us parents off against the other in turn, until all was confusion. This time they had been *my* contacts, but had met John and Jane briefly. We discovered later that this lady had occult-connections but, before her death, she made a deep, ongoing, fleshly impression on the life of one of our daughters.

So, by and large, our guardianship-question has not been an easy one to solve and, with three girls to take on in addition to their own largish families, it is very understandable. Guardians can mould and affect impressionable teenage-years more indelibly than parents who are thousands of miles away from their children most of the time. However, I would feel quite unable myself to be a guardian of other people's children. It is a task which requires much wisdom and spiritual-guidance, and is not to be undertaken lightly or sentimentally.

Susan, who had been born only fifteen months after her sister Anne, loathed *all* schooling, which she inherited from John, saying when she was small that she wanted only 'to be a Mummy', for which she must have felt absolutely no formal education was necessary at all! It was always difficult to take her back to school, even after short half-term breaks from Kenyan Prep School, because she was tearful and homesick. I empathised entirely, because at the age of five in England I myself tried the well-worn trick of asking permission to go to the cloakroom during lesson-time, grabbing my coat and walking home alone on dangerous, and even wintry, foggy main-roads, much to my mother's consternation. I really detested school in my earlier years but, contrarily, did not want to leave when the time came. I don't think I ever just wanted 'to be a Mummy', like Susan, but I certainly craved my Mother's attention and companionship, in vain.

Any second child born in quick succession to a first, and then followed even more rapidly by a third, can easily feel squashed, although in Susan's case she was very much wanted and loved by both parents. This may have caused her unconsciously to seek extra parental-attention by trying to remain behind at home, "to help you cook and look after Louise and Paul," she offered most convincingly. I felt very condemned when I was forced to refuse, explaining that school was compulsory, but I found parting from the girls at the beginning of term, or after half-term, doubly hard. It was not unknown for me to retreat to the car to sob after saying goodbye to the children, especially when it came to leaving them in England while we returned to Africa!

Paul was just coming up to two when we went to the UK on our first family leave, and three and a half when we went to England the next time. On this second occasion, we rented a furnished house that boasted a black and white TV. He would ask to have the morning children's programmes switched on and I would leave him watching while I hastened back to the kitchen to continue preparing the lunch. Often a little voice would be heard shouting, "Mummy, Mummy, come quickly, it's not Jesus. Please put it off!" I was amazed how, at such a young age, he sensed what was 'Jesus' and what was not! He was always correct. He was reacting to occult- practices and something below-standard, and had no wish to view, although they were supposed to be items of interest to toddlers. Could this be attributed largely to the fact that I had spent time daily, as I was bottle-feeding him, reading God's Word, meditating, praying in

114

English and, more importantly, in *tongues*? I believe that it is significant, and saw early evidence that his spirit was responding to the Holy Spirit through me and us, despite the fact that he could not have comprehended with his full understanding intellectually. Was the child, Samuel, of the Old Testament, something of a parallel?

Paul continued to be discerning when reading not-always-suitable library books, which is merciful because I never had time to vet these from cover-to-cover and had to trust the children's own judgment, after our teaching them the standards put forward in God's own Book.

In February 1977 it was necessary for me to have a major operation in Nairobi. In fact, it was one major, with a series of three minors, so was quite traumatic. Medical work is excellent in Nairobi, being private, with the cream of local and expatriate surgeons and very caring nursing for the most part. A lot of aftercare and convalescence was needed in my case, and it was decided that I should go to England for a complete break.

We looked into our finances and saw that, if I lived near to St. Brandon's School in Clevedon, Somerset, which the three oldest girls were attending and had them with me as day-girls, this would effect quite a saving in school-fees. Christian friends of Christian friends offered us their, as yet unused, retirement-home, a bus-ride from the school, and Susan and Julia came to stay with me for that summer-term, which was the one in which Susan had to sit her 'O'-level exams. I did not know that the Lord would use my time staying in Clevedon much later, and I found it a very pleasant residential area with many beautiful Victorian houses

Anne had, by this time, left school and had just completed a secretarial course elsewhere. She had known from the age of eleven that she wanted to nurse and be a midwife. None of the first three girls felt they could face, or needed, 'A'-levels and indeed, in the seventies, careers did not demand the higher-levels of education that they do today, due to there being far more potential employees than jobs.

I was able to get Anne a temporary post with the Müller Homes initially, caring for orphaned children, and later she worked in their Bristol bookshop until the time came around for her to begin nursing-training at Exeter. She has never, in fact, had cause to use the secretarial-skills she studied as a second-choice career possibility, but keyboard knowledge is useful for computer operation. She is every inch a senior community midwife now, and very dedicated to her work.

After Susan's exam and end-of-term, she, Julia and I flew back to Kenya for the summer-holidays, driving to the coast in August for our customary family-fortnight away. It was good to be home again! Also to be well once more.

13. Wives Submit; Husbands Love (Eph. 5:22-33)

All the inevitable strains and stresses of taking on board an instant family, calling for many adjustments for us all, plus my own frailty after a total of eleven medical operations, drove a wedge between John and I. He was never a good communicator and it was difficult to get his attention to talk and pray through problems. I seemed to lack what it took to cope with the many and varied demands on my time, and we began to quarrel, especially about the children. He did not actually compare me with Jane or his mother as such, but I felt as though I were being compared silently, and he did not appear to be totally convinced that I could only be me, warts and all, and could never be precisely like anyone else!

I sought the counsel of a number of mature Christians and ministers who tried to help and bring about a reconciliation, but to no lasting avail. Inevitably, but quite wrongly, I began to think about separation - not a legal one, and definitely not a divorce, but an initial time of being apart in the hope that absence would make the heart grow fonder and enable us to work through our difficulties.

I prayed and wept much, being utterly torn. One thing I could not face, however, was separation from the little boy I had brought up from ten weeks old, and Louise, from the age of four and a half. I asked John's permission to go and live in England, purchase a property and have Paul and Louise with me for state schooling there. Additionally, if he could not face living permanently in Britain, whether he would prayerfully consider coming to visit us during all school holidays, finance permitting.

117

Paul had started Prep School in Kenya one year earlier at the age of almost six, and loved it. He had greatly missed Louise when she began school at the age of five and three quarters and, in order to help him to wait until his time came round, we went out together most weeks and bought some item of school equipment, as a sort of 'school trousseau'. I had to guess at the size he would be then, and order name-tapes to sew on to each item, as that was all part of the fun of preparing. This 'trousseau-collecting' began when he was aged three and a half, and lasted for just over two years! Some weeks we might just buy a tube of toothpaste or a pair of shoelaces, to eke out the requirements to match the waiting-period, and then go and unlock his big, black metal school-trunk and he would place the named item in it with much tenderness and longing.

Since Paul and Louise were now happily settled together in one boarding-school, I could safely leave them to be taken good care of for one term while I went on to the UK to look for a house, furnish it and wait for John to bring them for the 1978 summer holidays.

My Aunty Amy's seaside flat in Kent was up for sale as by this time she had had to go into a nursing-home, but my parents advised me against purchase because one exterior wall to her bedroom had been condemned by the local authorities, with the threat of demolishing and changing its size and shape, due to its awkward protrusion near a road. Also my sister was living there at the time with her two children because her husband was living and working away from home, and this enabled my aunt to collect some rent pending the sale of the property.

John agreed to my having available the purchase-price of the flat, but it proved quite impossible to find a family-sized

118

house, in reasonable condition, for such a low figure, and he had specified that the house must be in the West Country, so my Aunt's flat in Kent was a non-starter. As it turned out, her flat would, in any case, have been far too small for us. Eventually I managed to find a detached house in Cornwall, which needed re-wiring and decorating, for one and a half times the sum he had allotted, which caused further problems in our relationship, and arguments and justifications flying to and fro in the post!

It should be remembered that John had left England in late 1949 to become a Kenya-settler, when prices in both the UK and Kenya were very different from those in the late seventies. He was not, therefore, really in a position to know just how much the cost of living had rocketed and could simply not understand how I could possibly have spent so much money on purchasing and putting the house in good order. In consequence, there were condemnatory mutterings of 'gross extravagance' for a long time to come. People who had lived for years in Britain felt, on the other hand, that I had done ample justice to the sum expended, but not John! Even in Kenya, he was oblivious to the cost of living, particularly the price of groceries, which he was not involved in buying.

By this time we had put three girls through Kenyan and UK boarding-schools with escalating fees, expensive uniform, and had flown them to and from Kenya for most holidays. Louise and Paul were still at their fee-paying private boarding school in Kenya, of course, and all our non-index linked income from investments, originating from John's family-legacies, were no longer realistic and we were beginning to feel the pinch. This was one of my main reasons for sensing that in future our remaining children would be forced to attend UK state schools.

119

Thus, many of our arguments and disagreements now centred around money matters, which is apparently the most common reason for breakdown of marriages. I had lived in England longer and more recently than John, so was less shocked by the rapid rise in the cost of living than he was. In Kenya I had always handled all household-bills, with the exception of rent, electricity and rates, all of which were still relatively low-priced.

I hoped that our separation between April and July 1978 would have gone a long way to repairing the breach, and felt excited as I drove to the Cornish airfield to collect John, Paul and Louise from the plane in my second-hand Peugeot 204 Estate, for which John had given me a purchase allowance.

I was really glad to see them *all* but noticed with horror how pale and gaunt John was, and the fact that his trousers were just hanging around his waist. Had he been pining, I wondered. I probably looked much the same myself, with all the house-hunting, moving and furnishing I had had to cope with alone, plus some typewriter examination-marking I had undertaken to bring in a little income. With all this, I had not had much time on my hands in which consciously to pine but, yes, I had missed my family, and my little boy had grown quite tall, as had Louise, who was becoming increasingly attractive with her dark, curly hair and big, brown eyes.

I tried to extract a promise from John that he would allow me to keep Louise and Paul in England and school them free of charge at two good, local state-schools. He refused, typically, to give me an outright answer, and this made for more tension between us. Meanwhile, the children began to enjoy England more and more, and pleaded to be allowed to stay. The lovely Cornish beaches were just a drive away, and the summer weather was quite good that year.

In Kenya it had become difficult latterly to know how on earth to give them any kind of recreation, as outings were becoming increasingly expensive, and suitable places for European children tricky to come by. Some beauty spots could be dangerous also. They both felt they had had enough of Africa for the time being and wanted now to feel they fitted in with those of the same cultural background.

Spiritually errant, I went to a solicitor to obtain a legal separation from John, with custody of the two children who adamantly did not wish to return to Africa with John. The reason for the first was merely a means to achieve the latter. I acted entirely after the flesh, and deeply regret now going to those lengths, and have since repented.

John was humiliated that evening when someone called on behalf of my solicitor to warn John that I had taken out an indictment against him, preventing him from leaving England's shores with the children. He was also furious with me! However, this goaded him to employ a Christian lawyer who, somewhat unusually, decided that our marriage had potential.

They called together a meeting with my solicitor, plus the two of us, and we hammered out in private all the problems. They counselled that a reconciliation take place, the children remain in the UK and we drop the case! Where the church seemed to have failed us or we, as believers, had not followed scriptural-teaching, here were two solicitors, out of court, getting somewhere at last! We both feared divorce and knew it to be wrong. Could the love we had felt so strongly for each other only a few years ago really have died so soon? Had the Lord changed? Had His call altered in any way?

We took a few days' holiday after this at a seaside-resort and, to my relief, John agreed to leave the children with me, but could in no way promise that he would ever come permanently to live with us in the UK. The children were elated to know that they could remain in England.

We felt somewhat bereft when he left us, but he was due to visit again the following Christmas, so we had that to look forward to and plan. The children duly started at the local junior and secondary schools respectively, began to settle well, cope with an exceedingly cold, English winter, and even enjoy the snow. The house was already double-glazed when I bought it and, by adding extra wall-mounted, flued gas heaters, we kept very snug, cosy and happy together. John liked the house and garden, and he had a small study upstairs with a telephone extension, but he had always found it hard to demonstrate approval or gratitude.

I began teaching typewriting privately at home, using an insulated, electrically-heated, wooden summerhouse down the garden as a classroom, but we were really too far West to make this work pay, there being virtually no vacancies in local offices for typists.

John visited us again at Christmas, and it actually snowed on Christmas Eve itself, giving us a traditional Christmas-card scene as we looked out of the window at several inches of crisp, virgin snow on Christmas Morning. After church, we enjoyed a home-cooked turkey lunch and, in the afternoon, all wrapped up snugly and went out for a walk so that the children could make a snowman. Paul was not quite so happy, however, once the snow began to melt and penetrate the seams of his Vinyl gloves!

The holidays passed quickly and it was soon time both for the children to return to school and for John to fly back to Kenya. I had come to the conclusion that I could have gone on quite contentedly with this pattern of John visiting us during school-holidays, if he really could not face living in the UK permanently. We managed to maintain a better relationship for the few weeks he spent with us each time, and it was cheaper for one person to fly to and fro rather than several.

John returned to Kenya via Amsterdam in January (1979) and, to my amazement, telephoned me from a Dutch hotel to say that his onward-flight had been postponed and he only wished it were possible for me to be with him! I suddenly found myself feeling very lonely and missing him, wishing also we could have been together ... anywhere!

I pulled myself together and got on with daily-living and private-teaching. Even so, I had not bargained for the bombshell that he was to drop the very next month. He wrote me an aerogramme informing me that it was neither right nor scriptural for us to continue living apart for most of the year, that he had no intention of coming to England to live, nor to visit at Easter, and that I must submit to him as the head of the home and as my husband, whether or not I felt like it, and return to Kenya immediately with the two children!

The children and I were confused and devastated, feeling we could no longer cope with Africa's corruption and loneliness. Louise was particularly upset and often in tears, and Paul was hoping that Daddy would change his mind. They wanted him to be with us, but not in Africa! I sought once again prayer and counsel, and confided in a local Christian couple who were preparing to serve the Lord in Israel and whose fellowship I had come to appreciate. The wife showed me from scripture what I already knew only too well - that I must obey my husband, and had no choice but to do the Lord's bidding and his.

All my reactions rebelled inwardly against returning to Africa. I had become used and acclimatised to life in England and being a member of a 'normal' Baptist church, and found it altogether more conducive for the children and myself. They were happy and doing well at school, and had not the slightest desire to return to Kenya and have yet another change in their lives and schooling.

However, I had no peace until I agreed, and determined to show the Lord that I meant business by booking three air passages to Nairobi, leaving me only nine overfull days in which to put the house and car on the market, sell house-contents, pay household bills and pack umpteen suitcases, etc. I had purposely chosen not to delay, lest I should change my mind and disobey John's instructions! But, yes, I did have peace and had, of course, known all along that it was not right in the Lord's eyes for us to be apart.

I was amazed at the lack of condemnation from the Lord Himself. He had abundantly blessed and provided for the children and I and we lacked nothing, except a normal, two-parent home life. But then the Lord never condemns, although He may gently challenge and judge, fairly and in love, unlike so many of us human beings.

I have since come to see that while divorce is, in most cases, scripturally wrong (fornication and the unbelieving-partner departing being two indisputable reasons for possible divorce - Matt. 5:32 and I Cor. 7:15), there is also a case for both sides agreeing to stay apart for a brief time (compare I Cor. 7:5). There can be much value in a couple who have ceased being able to communicate civilly with each other, who can nevertheless trust each other implicitly not to have any alternative relationship, to have a short period apart, and then express their individual problems and contentions in writing to each other. John always found it easier to write than say how he felt, and actively avoided all forms of confrontation, however mild, especially passive ones. He could not communicate completely with anyone and had never formed close friendships.

John and I could most emphatically trust each other to be 100% faithful. There never had been any question of another person in the background at any time, on either side. John and I did write at length to each other during these months, but it was difficult, if not impossible, for him to put himself in my shoes as the only non-blood relative in the family, the step-parent and the general-scapegoat. Men tend, by nature, to be less sensitive than women and less ready to see where they might be wrong and apologise. Our separation was never right, but perhaps it achieved something long-term.

I felt so guilty about John reacting to money spent on the house that I made a further mistake in arranging to fly back with the two children by cheap charter-flight via the Sudan. We all found the long flying and stopover hours very tiring and difficult, especially as I was unable to get the children a drink while we stood waiting several hours in the in-transit lounge at Khartoum Airport.

The toilets at the airport were also indescribably filthy, and there was no water, so we were unable to freshen up for the

125

next leg of the journey to Nairobi. The only advantage was quite a big saving on fares! I found it disconcerting and confusing to be told by John that there was absolutely no need whatever to have economised on fares and that, whatever it cost, I could have travelled by direct flight! Money was suddenly no object, but I had not known that.

Not long after we returned to our home in Kenya, John brightly announced one day to me that he felt it was perhaps time that we returned *permanently* to the UK! Was I imagining things, or did he actually say *permanently*? "But why on earth did we have to come all this way to hear this?" I wailed at him, on the verge of tears and quite unable to take in all the ramifications of what he was really saying.

By now the house I had purchased in England, and had worked so hard on, had been sold, having been left in the capable hands of the estate-agent who had sold it to me in the first place. It sold for a good price and most of the expenditure had been warranted and recovered, but one can never sell household-effects for the prices one paid for them, because they are used. That was the main area of inevitable loss. John felt that particular house was, in any case, too far West for him personally, despite his having chosen the very town in which it was situated (because it was where Susan, who now wished to be called Sue, was based at the time), but he now desired to return to roost in his native East Devon, if he must live in England at all! For him, it was almost tantamount to emigrating after living in Africa for so long.

I went through quite a lot of resentment and self-pity because he had, in fact, brought the children and me over 4,000 miles back to Kenya in order for me to undertake, solo, all the

126

selling and packing up that was required, neither being John's forte. In fact, I came to realise over the years that John hated all kinds of packing, even to pack for one night away from home, and would stall and procrastinate until the last minute or beyond. This may well be connected with his deep loathing of being sent away to various kinds of educational-establishments from a young age, and the agonising homesickness and insecurity it produced.

John's announcement meant that the children had to change schools twice more: once in Kenya, using a more locally-situated school where they could be weekly boarders and come home for weekends, which they enjoyed; then again, a term and a half later, when we left Kenya in July 1979 to move back to England.

Louise had always been a particularly easy and adaptable child and she weathered these storms relatively well, but Paul took time to adjust to each new situation and, understandably, his schooling suffered somewhat in each first term. However, once school in England was familiar and we were all together as a family, he made rapid progress and was two years ahead in English alone, due to the excellent foundation he had first received at Kenya Prep School, and becoming a most avid reader from the age of four, when he learnt to read fluently as a nursery school-child.

There was a lighter side to all the work and trauma of selling and packing up in Kenya. One old, wizened African woman came with a group of others, who had heard that there was a sale at our house. I tried patiently to take her all around to see what was on show, only to have her say at the end of it all, "Yes, I see. Now I will just buy those two safety pins for twenty

127

cents!" In fact, her words summed up a whole attitude here in Africa which made me vow never to have such sales again. Most literally do come simply "to see", case the joint and even steal goods placed out on show, and this also was so on that occasion. It is much safer to employ an agent to sell for you, although he must take his commission, of course.

Perhaps 'tragic' more aptly describes another event, rather than 'funny'. An American, ordained missionary from a nearby town drove out to see what was on offer in our sale and, because he was a servant of the Lord, John agreed to come way down in the price of certain items, which we were both surprised interested him as he had been in Africa a long time and had an established family-home. However, on going to the auctioneers in Nairobi a little later to deposit a number of the more valuable items we had to sell, imagine our shocked amazement to find the very goods we had sold very cheaply to this minister were on display in the auctioneer's showroom! When John challenged him, he just laughed and said he went in for this sort of buying and selling "for a bit of fun!" We failed to share his sense of amusement or self-justification. We lost heavily over that wheeling and dealing, and felt disappointed at being cheated by a fellow-missionary. But we had once more to practise what we taught, and to forgive up to seventy times seven, and remember that we ourselves may not err in that area, but we are very far from perfect, as our recent separation had proved.

Before leaving Kenya we flew to, and spent a very relaxing week on, the shores of Lake Baringo. I was so tired after selling and packing that I benefited greatly from that holiday where we were waited on hand and foot. Louise also learnt to swim in the Club pool.

Our cat, Smokey, who was by now getting on for seven years old, had to go to the excellent local Blue Cross Kennels and Cattery in order to have essential vaccinations and arrangements made for her separate air travel to the UK and then six months' quarantine. The plan was that she should fly ahead of us to reduce the waiting-time to collect her again in our new UK home, but an extended UK postal-strike delayed the necessary import-permit's arrival for several weeks, so that she left considerably later than we did, only prolonging the suffering all round.

14. Return unto the Land of Thy Fathers (Gen. 31:3)

After our return to the UK in 1979 I felt as though I must be becoming something of an expert in selling, packing, house-buying and reselling! But we were concerned, as July turned to August and the nights began to get chillier, that we needed to be settled quickly in order to know to which schools to send the children early in September. Apart from all that, it was essential to acquire a permanent roof over our heads.

We were camping, on a friend's advice, near Kentisbeare, Cullompton, Devon, and heard excellent reports of the junior and secondary schools at a large village, with some light industry, called Uffculme, not very far away. Therefore, we began specifically searching for a family-sized dwelling in or near to Uffculme, and ended up buying a 'Devon longhouse' in the village of Uffculme itself.

The children thoroughly enjoyed living in this house which, I might add, was more than *twice* the price of the house I had bought previously in the UK! But it was more spacious, and had been built in the Georgian era and style.

The recommended local schools more than lived up to their reputation, the secondary school being an ex-grammar school which had had the same headmaster for many years and kept up high standards and good discipline. Louise quickly made friends, as usual, and was happy and well-adjusted, making excellent progress all the way through that school in the A-stream.

Paul attended the local junior school, which was only half a minute's walk diagonally across from our house, the

130

nearness making him feel extra secure. It took him slightly longer to settle, but he was very happy there, and in the village as a whole. "After all," he reasoned, "the fish and chip shop here is just as near as it was when we lived in England before!"

We greatly enjoyed walks and drives in the very beautiful surrounding Devon and Somerset countryside. We often visited local National Trust gardens also. The biggest difficulty proved to be one that is very typical nowadays, especially for ex-missionaries: finding a church nearby which was really going somewhere spiritually, and was not just turned in on itself.

We seemed to spend most of the next four years searching and testing, not looking for the perfect church, yet never feeling totally at home or fulfilled in any that we attended. We even committed to a large, charismatic housechurch many miles away for about seventeen months, but we were disappointed at the lack of prayer and outreach, and found too strong a reliance upon spoken prophecy by way of guidance, some of which tended to be subjective or only full of very positive blessings and provisions from the Lord, many of them not coming to fruition because of imbalance and a lack of completely lining up with God's *written* Word.

We wound up at the small, village Baptist Church eventually, and John was invited to preach in another Baptist chapel on the Somerset-Devon border, with a view to becoming its non-ordained pastor. However, the church was already split over the charismatic issue and, in fact, was completely dissolved not long afterwards, with its buildings put up for sale, so that appointment, by God's mercy, did not come our way.

We were trying to push ajar a few spiritual doors, naturally, and, prior to all this, we had wondered whether the

131

Lord might be calling us to serve Him in France. But, after giving this a fair test, and John finding at his age that he could only put sentences together in French with extreme slowness and difficulty, to say nothing of a lack of pastoral gifting, we realised that the door was being opened no further to us, although there were very real needs to fulfil in the Brittany area where we spent a summer and Christmas holiday, partly to test a possible call there.

In 1981 we put our house on the market in order to try to buy something more modern, manageable and economical, but it was to be two and a half years before it sold. We tended to go along with the estate-agents' valuation rather than specifically asking the Lord what *His* fair price was. We had added a downstairs guest-room by converting a covered yard between the external back wall of our sitting-room and one wall of the garage, for which we had, of course, to obtain local council approval. This augmented the sale value but, after two years of showing umpteen people around the house and keeping it in doubly pristine condition to impress, we took time out particularly to bring the subject of our unsold property before the Lord. "Were we meant to stay in it, rather than move elsewhere, and trust You for the shortfall in our income?" we petitioned the Lord. And then He showed us that it was overpriced and gave us an exact figure at which to offer it for sale!

The Lord quickly confirmed that this was *His* price by sending an engaged couple along, one week later at nine o'clock on a summer's evening, who were immediately taken with the Georgian exterior, let alone the interior, and the young man was talking to John of buying it for the agreed price while still outside in the small, front garden! Once they had come inside and viewed all round they were even more convinced that they should buy it, and within six weeks all formalities had been completed. We therefore moved out, and they moved in, taking over all existing curtains, carpets, and a number of appliances and other items besides, which was to our mutual advantage.

The morning following this couple's initial viewing of the property we began earnestly asking the Lord where *He* wanted us to live, and how *He* wanted us to serve Him. This was by no means the first time, of course, but one cannot actually move to another house before the first is sold, so we had merely prayed and window-shopped previously.

During the previous year we had heard a tape by Steve Lightle, an American Messianic Jew, entitled 'Exodus II', and then read his book with the same title. Through these and a local couple, the Lord had begun involving us more in intercession for the Jewish people and their return from the Diaspora to The Promised Land. This interest had begun for me in 1980 at a Lydia Conference.

One day in 1983, while John was in the bath, he told the Lord rather casually, "Well, Lord, You can send us back to Kenya, if You wish!" He omitted to tell *me* about this conversation but, somewhere around the time of this buyer-couple coming on the scene, I myself felt impressed by the Lord to be willing to return to Kenya. His astounding prophetic call this time was, "Go back to Kenya and be involved in Exodus II of the Jewish people from The Diaspora." I found myself rather amazed by my own surrender, as things had changed adversely for us in Kenya even before we left, let alone now, some four years later, and I could not see what Kenya had to do with the

133

return of Jews to Israel. It made no sense. I was also wondering how to share this with John and check it against his guidance, but need not have worried. When eventually I summoned up the courage to do so, he smiled and said that was precisely how he felt the Lord had been speaking to him, also. I think Jesus, as He sat at His Father's right hand interceding for us, must have chortled as He said to Father something after the order of, "Here we go *again,* Abba!"

However, we felt we should seek prayer support and confirmation on this matter, so drafted a prayer letter to key Christian friends, asking them to wait on the Lord with and for us about this. The general consensus of spiritual opinion was, "Yes, it adds up; we feel it *is* right."

Back I went to the old pattern of selling, packing and house-moving once more. We gradually eliminated everything but bare essentials, but the day came when they too had to be packed and sent off to the forwarding-agents. A local Christian couple kindly let us part of their furnished and equipped guest-wing, which we used mainly for sleeping, while going to and from the house to continue all our preparations to return to Kenya.

Smokey became her usual unsettled self as she realised we were packing up once again. Like most animals, she was sensitive to all changes, particularly any which would unsettle her. Since we came to and from the house until almost the last minute, she was able to have company all day, most days, be fed and watered, and stay put at night in the house. However, when we completed all that had to be done, we drove Smokey to a cattery deep in the Devon countryside and arranged for the owner to keep her until departure day. We could not take her to our friends' guest-wing, since they had four yappy little dogs and she would have been petrified. We took her bedding and food dishes to the cattery and asked the owner kindly to stick rigidly to Smokey's normal diet. We hated parting with her, even temporarily, but at least we did not have to put her into quarantine on arrival in Kenya, as we had done in England in 1979.

Louise finished her 'O'-levels that summer and then went to help at a Müller's Children's Day-Care centre on the Somerset coast for the rest of the holidays, prior to starting her two year 'A'-level course in Devon, during which she boarded at the local Manse.

Julia had completed her training as a Nursery Nurse a couple of years earlier and she had herself returned to Kenya to work as a teacher of two-to-three year olds at the then Trinity Fellowship nursery school on the outskirts of Nairobi. Julia was on leave in the UK that summer, so we saw something of her before our departure.

A Kenyan pastor-friend of John's, whom he had known for eighteen years (and, in fact, the very man who had tried unsuccessfully to exorcise our haunted house in Kenya) had written to say he was now pastoring eight new churches in Kenya's Western Province, and invited John to come and join him. I personally had grave doubts and discernment about this man's character, but John saw his invitation as the only positive straw to cling to on returning to Kenya, yet I was burdened that this opening did not appear to match the Lord's call to be involved in 'Exodus II'. Here was yet another case when I had to submit to John while not being able to agree with him, and leave the Lord to overrule.

135

15. Pray for the Peace of Jerusalem

To go back a little chronologically, I was attending a Lydia conference on intercession in the North of England in May 1980 that the Lord spoke unmistakeably to me to begin interceding for the Jewish people, both in Israel and the Diaspora. I began to read as much as I could, because I knew very little about Israel, had never been there, and had had limited contact with Jews up to that point.

Some time after I had begun praying for the Jewish people Louise gave us first a tape, then a book entitled 'Exodus II' by Steve Lightle, as mentioned in the previous chapter. No sooner had I heard the tape and read the book than I was quite unable to get its message out of my system. The author, a Messianic, American-Jew, received a vision from the Lord in August 1974 during a time of prayer and fasting in Brunswick, West Germany, which he believed revealed God's plan to bring nearly three million Jews out of the Soviet Union and return them to Israel. In clear, picture-form, Steve saw thousands of Jewish people streaming out of Russia on a Highway specially prepared for them. The Lord went on to show him that He would raise up Moses' ministries, as in the first exodus out of Egypt, to confront Russia's Pharaoh with the command, 'Thus, saith the Lord God of Israel, "Let My people go."' As on the first occasion, this would lead to refusal, and the Lord's consequent prophetic plagues and judgments upon that nation, until it was willing to 'vomit up' the Jews.

The portion of the Highway which Steve saw at that time went through Poland and, in particular, the city of Warsaw;

136

then into East Germany via Berlin; through Helmstat and into Brunswick - the exact place where this vision was received, and which had been the very seat of Naziism - and on to Hanover and Holland, where the Jews boarded ships which took them to Israel.

God confirmed this vision from a number of scriptures, but notably Is. 35:8-10 - the Highway of Holiness. Since then, the Lord has revealed additional different routes that this Highway will take, affecting several nations and, amazingly, He has called His Christian people, quite independently one of the other, to begin to make spiritual and physical preparations for this Exodus. Some are called only to help pray this second exodus into being; others are involved in farming, harvesting and storing grains; others have beef on the hoof or fish in vast ponds; others have accommodation and transport at the ready, while yet others are keeping medicines, clothing, footwear and Bibles in Russian and Hebrew.

It is impossible to recount all, but it is easy to obtain a copy of this book and read the story personally, checking all the relevant scriptures as one goes along. ISBN 0917726561. Suffice it to say that I did this first and, considerably later, John followed suit, each of us going through the Bible with a toothcomb to test the accuracy of what might otherwise seem some crackpot story! The Lord amply confirmed to us every word, and also showed us that *we* too were to have some part in Exodus II, which would begin with intercession and keeping closely abreast with news and events affecting Jews in the Diaspora.

We felt so helpless, so ignorant! What did either of us know, for example, of the Jewish people or the Soviet Union?

137

School history and geography lessons had not touched on either of these subjects in any detail. And how could returning to Kenya possibly fulfil *this* call? Could we have misheard, misunderstood? We decided that before we returned to Kenya we must, therefore, begin by visiting Israel. We thought it should be simple enough to take an air stopover, Israel being approximately half-way between Britain and Kenya, but this proved too expensive and it was, unbelievably, much cheaper to go first to Israel and back, and then separately to Kenya. In any case, Paul, then aged twelve, was not interested in joining us in Israel, and our cat, Smokey, now aged eleven, needed to travel on the same direct aircraft as we, in order to be classified as 'excess baggage' and have her cat basket put in the special hold beneath the passenger cabin. Paul went to stay with Devonian friends who had a smallholding, and three sons for company, while John and I took a ten-day trip to Israel.

As soon as our plane touched down in Tel Aviv, we felt strangely at home, as if we belonged, and were every bit as Jewish as the Israelis! Did not the Apostle Paul say in Romans 2:28-29, 'For he is not a Jew, which is one outwardly; but he is a Jew, which is one inwardly …'

We owe everything as Christians to the Jews. Our Old Testament is entirely Jewish and our New Testament is written mainly by Jews, to say nothing of the fact that our Messiah (and theirs) was Jewish, born, brought up and having ministered only in the land of Israel. One Christian lady-tourist, carrying an enormous Bible in her hand as she was shown around various sites in Israel, was absolutely amazed to hear that Jesus was a Jew, and found it extremely hard to come to terms with the fact! This only goes to prove what appalling ignorance one can have,

138

as a Christian, of the Bible, for Jesus was, is and always will be, 'King of the Jews'.

If we felt we belonged in Tel Aviv, when we reached the beautiful city of Jerusalem we were able to echo the words of the Psalmist in Ps. 102:13-14, 'Thou shalt arise, and have mercy upon Zion, for the time to favour her, yea, the set time is come. For thy servants take pleasure in her stones, and favour the dust thereof'. We never recalled feeling exactly like this in Africa in her regular dry-seasons, when the earth turns to powder and gets into everything, yet here we were literally loving every particle of her dust and stones! And it is always the Jews who think we are quite potty because of the extent of our love for them and … imagine, even the dust of Jerusalem! "You just have to be Jewish," they all say, "to love us so much."

We spent a week in Jerusalem and were booked into an Arab hotel at Bethany (now Abu Dis) which we had entirely to ourselves. Mealtimes could be as flexible as we needed them to be, and we found that the very adequate Israeli breakfast and generous evening meal meant that we could just take half-board (bed, breakfast and evening meal) and that at lunchtime it was cheap and easy to buy freshly baked bread, cheese and fruit, etc, to consume wherever we happened to be. No one minded if we decided to eat it in our hotel bedroom, prior to taking a siesta.

We walked, or took local Arab or Jewish buses, and linked up with expatriate Christians working in Jerusalem, and their help and information was to prove invaluable for the future. Money was short, so expensive, guided tours were out, but an elderly Christian friend very generously offered to drive us down to Lake Galilee and back for the day. We had a super time, having places pointed out to us by one who was a real expert on Israel, and stopping to sightsee en route. We had lunch at a beautiful lakeside kibbutz (co-operative) restaurant. Our host was exceedingly amusing and entertaining, as well as informative, and we had an unforgettable day as we enjoyed his company and fellowship together in the Lord.

After our week in Jerusalem, John and I went on to the Mediterranean town of Netanya. He enjoyed swimming in the warm, August sea, but the coastline is unbearably humid at this time of year and, while very attractive, it did not match Jerusalem for us, although it was very hot there also. Netanya was swarming with French-speaking North African and local resident Jews, and I found my knowledge of French far more useful in shops and elsewhere than English!

So, our first taste of Israel was over and we had to get back to Devon, collect our thoughts, Paul, Smokey and our belongings, and go all the way back to Heathrow for our flight to Nairobi, Kenya, to which Paul was much looking forward, loving, as he did, all air travel, for a reason which mystified me! I find whistling through the air in a metal tube decidedly boring and tiring, and my one interest is simply to arrive at my destination!

A Christian friend drove us, cat and luggage, to the airport. Smokey decided that she was not going to suffer the indignity of staying in a cage, and began to yowl incessantly when first put in it. She clearly wanted out and to come and sit on my lap and, as we had previously purchased a harness and lead for a miniature dog, it was safe for her to wear this and sit with me in the front passenger-seat. Once she had marched all around the front of the car, she duly settled down on my lap and went fast asleep!

140

I was a little anxious about her going into the plane's hold, so the Chief Steward kindly escorted John and me to the portion of the hold where her basket would be put. We worried a little about the noise of the engines, but at least they would drown all the yowling and, on a ten-hour, direct flight, she would presumably soon become tired and even hoarse!

We need not have been concerned for, after landing at dawn on 4th September 1983, 'Madam's' cage was unloaded from the hold but she was not subjected to the further trauma of being put on a conveyor belt with everyone's baggage. When we had collected our cases, we had to enquire her whereabouts, produce her documentation, and found her well and happy.

To avoid yet further yowling, chirruping loud greetings of "Mrrow" through the fine mesh-door of her cat-basket, I took Smokey out, put on her harness and lead, and she behaved impeccably as we passed through Customs, strutting up and down the Customs' check-out as if she owned the place, and enchanting Customs' Officers and passengers alike. At last Smokey was 'home' and would not have to demand the artificial warmth of a gas fire, as in an English winter. *This* climate was sensible, with none of that cold, white substance that fell in England that she had to shake off her paws and coat with disgust! Speaking Swahili, we greeted all airport staff with whom we had to do, and did not even have to open our luggage, let alone pay any customs' duty, and no one checked Smokey's harness for drugs or jewels!

We were *back*! "Happy, Darling?" John asked me, and I had to admit I was, yet I continued to sense no inward peace about working with John's pastor-friend up-country, nor could I see the slightest connection in so doing with Israel, the Jews and

Exodus II still. However, before we could go anywhere and take up any spiritual work, our personal papers had to be put in order, unaccompanied baggage cleared and collected from the airport within the next week or so, purchases made and, last but not least, a suitable school found for Paul immediately.

Our daughter, Julia, had a middle-aged European friend who had gone on UK leave who wanted to sub-let her house during her absence, so the Lord wonderfully provided us with a two-bedroomed house and her worker for about a month, quite near to where Julia lived on the outskirts of Nairobi, while we coped with all the preamble.

That month provided us with the opportunity to have a day of prayer and fasting specifically to seek the Lord as to why we had returned, insofar as His work - our No 1 priority - was concerned. I recalled yet again that the Lord had told us in England that somehow we would be involved with the *Jewish* people and Exodus II, but all this continued to seem as remote as ever. What did Kenya, of all places, have to do with either, we wondered? This day, set aside to seek the Lord, revealed no further light on working alongside the up-country pastor. On that subject, the heavens were as brass.

From Batya's Photo Album

Batya's parents

Batya's wedding

Wedding Day

Early marriage days Nakuru Kenya

Smokey - cat on a hot tin roof

Our haunted house, Lanet

All the Fulcher girls, Nakuru 1972

Ethiopian - Jewish immigrant family, TSFAT, Israel 1993

Batya and John

Friends in Johannesburg

Passover Seder, South Africa

The family. John's memorial reception.
Weston-super-Mare.

16. A Troubled Fountain and a Corrupt Spring (Prov. 25:126)

Paul needed urgent admission to the right secondary school, since term was already under way. We researched most of the suitable schools in Nairobi which offered British university 'O' and 'A'-levels and settled, at last, on one at Langata, some seven miles from the city-centre. This was a day-school, so guardians had to be found to house and care for Paul in our absence up-country. This tugged heavily at my heart-strings, and probably at Paul's also.

Having established Paul both in school and in the home of his guardians (parents of two boys who attended the same school, and a Christian family), we drove to Western Province in the October in order to spend a week with the person under whose auspices we were due to work. We certainly received a very warm welcome when we finally arrived in the dark. A number of neighbours, on hearing that European visitors had arrived, came, as always, to extend their greetings. We were then fed, and retired gratefully to bed, after such a long day and arduous journey.

As the days went by, I felt a tremendous spiritual darkness and heaviness on that plot, yet when we visited a lovely, saved, local Baptist family nearby, comprising parents and no less than twelve children, the spiritual air was totally different!

Half way through our week's stay, our pastor-friend announced that we would have to move out of his house (having already invited us to come for a week), as his children were rather cramped in the verandah-storeroom, but that the

143

Baptist neighbour had a small, empty house on his plot which he was happy for us to use free of rent. We thought this request rather odd, but later it was to make sense.

Our pastor-friend accompanied us around a couple of his so-called out-churches, but there was a distant sort of attitude toward him by the local pastor and church members, which seemed peculiar. We also attended the church which met on his own plot on Sunday mornings, with most of the small congregation inviting themselves for lunch after the service, which must have been a challenge for our friend's wife as there was no income at that stage, and they already had four children.

At the end of the week, still all I could sense was darkness and foreboding, with absolutely no peace at all to return and work with this man. John felt I was just prejudiced because this man and I had never really hit it off. I never had proof of his genuineness and, in all the years that we had known him, he had never once, prior to this, even suggested John visit him. It had always been his visiting us, with the hope that John would reimburse him his fare and add a monetary gift, which was really tantamount to paying him to come to fast and pray with us!

However, peace or no peace, God's Word told me to submit to my husband and *he* felt it was right and, in any case, the only obvious door to spiritual ministry, and that we must return to Western Province to live. So, once more, we went house-hunting in the company of our friend, whose distant relative found us a brand new bungalow in the throes of completion and being painted. It was agreed that we could rent it, and that all the work would be finished by the time we were due to move in.

144

Off we went back to Nairobi to arrange the transportation of our effects up-country. I was feeling so miserable about living in Western Province, and so lacking inner peace about working with this particular person, that I asked the Pentecostal minister-friend, who had married us and who was visiting Kenya with his wife at that time, to pray for me. He was staying with the missionaries with whom our daughter, Julia, was working - Elisabeth and Godfrey Dawkins of Trinity Fellowship - who, in turn, invited us to their regular Thursday evening Bible study and prayer meeting. Our minister-friend had discerned needs in the gathering, and I felt I had a sackful which I was carting about on my back.

After being prayed for at that meeting, I can't say that I relished the thought of all that lay ahead any more, but I had surrendered my will to the Lord and invited Him to have His way and to overrule.

Moving-day dawned, but some last minute-business delayed John in town, and we did not leave Nairobi until midday, arriving weary and worn outside our new house after dark only to discover, to our horror, that a couple with a baby and some other female relatives were firmly ensconced inside and, like Luke's story of the importunate neighbour, the husband of the couple said words to the effect, "Trouble me not; the door is now shut, and my child is with me in bed; I cannot rise and give thee!" It was, in our case, pointless asking, seeking and knocking, as in the same Bible story (Luke 11:5-10) - at least not *that* night!

Western Province is particularly renowned for superstition and all forms of the occult. No one had really believed we were actually going to move in on the day agreed

145

with the landlord, and someone had to guard the house by living in it, so here they were - relations of the landlord.

By now it was getting quite late. In the car we had our cat Smokey plus a new animal acquisition called Rex, who was a predominantly black and tan German Shepherd, crossed with some other dubious canine species, which had resulted in his having a white blob on his chest and the tip of his tail. On the journey, John had stopped the car to fill up in Nakuru, when Rex suddenly jumped from the boot of the car to the front, where Smokey was happily sitting on my lap. She was not used to dogs and was extremely scared, so spat, hissed and swore at him while entrenching all of her front claws firmly into my scalp, forehead, face and neck. Blood was cascading down on to my clothing, and a horrified petrol-attendant winced and gingerly asked me what the matter was! With Smokey still clinging on for dear life, I would have thought it was all too obvious! Those claw-marks lasted for weeks, and I felt rather foolish as shopkeepers gave me puzzled looks. Perhaps they suspected I had been in a fight with my husband, wife-beating being very common in Africa.

"Well darling, there is only one thing for it - we shall have to book in at the local tourist hotel," I said to John. "And what on earth are we going to do with these two?" John asked himself as much as me, referring to Smokey and Rex. Mercifully, the European Hotelier himself was there, and we explained our predicament. "No problem," he reassured us, "you can park right in front of the room I have in mind for you, chain the dog up on its verandah and have the cat in your room, if you have no objection. And while you are unpacking, I will arrange for some supper for you both, and scrounge around for some food and

146

drink for both animals. I think I have a carton in my office that will make a good litter-tray for the cat!"

We were overwhelmed at his thoughtfulness and kindness, and he was as good as his word, even scrambling around the hotel gardens for some dry earth for Smokey's dirt-box! This town at least had hotel service in its favour, if little else!

Next morning we again pitched up at *our* house, importunity all at the ready, only to find, much to our relief, that the birds had flown earlier on. However, we were dumbfounded, in the light of day, to discover that the building-jobs and painting had hardly been *started,* let alone finished! In fact, almost nothing had been added or changed since we viewed the house. The landlord, having failed to get a further loan from his employer, had very typically run out of cash and was waiting for *our* month's rent in advance to pay the workmen for what little they had already done before they were willing to take up their tools once more. Also, he had the usual, fatalistic attitude, "Well, they might change their minds and not come!" Spain is not alone in its proverbial policy of 'Tomorrow, tomorrow'! One finds it all over Africa also.

Our effects arrived the next day, with all the workmen everywhere, inside and out, making it impossible to sort and unpack our belongings and, in any case, there was not one single fitted cupboard provided in which to put anything. We decided on two forms of strategy: to withhold all rent and use it to pay the workmen ourselves to complete, or even start, essential work inside the house; to live in one room at a time, as each was completed, until all were finished under our close supervision.

We had to go out and purchase basic furniture, since all we had were canvas garden chairs. We began with a kitchen table and a food-safe, and ordered beds for ourselves which took the carpenter an incredible two weeks to make! Meanwhile, we washed the cement floor of our bedroom and made up beds on that, using inflatable mattresses.

Furniture was very reasonably priced, since there were umpteen local carpenters, some of whom made furniture on shop-premises. John also went to a market some distance away and acquired two cane-settees to match some cane-chairs we had managed to purchase extremely cheaply, or been given by one of the outchurches.

Slowly, slowly, we got the rooms into decorative order and I began making curtains and covers by hand, which was a laborious task, and we bought inexpensive, local furniture to fill the voids. I had to sew mainly by daylight, as the electricity had never been connected, and I found it caused eyestrain to sew by oil-lamp at night. I also got a local carpenter to make up simple wardrobe-frames and I made curtains to hide their contents.

One missing item was a bath. A crude metal shower-head swung precariously aloft in what was meant to be the bathroom, and it actually had piped cold water, *when* the local authorities deigned to pump it our way, but John and I never felt really clean unless we *sat* in a bathtub, however shallow the water. I remembered how, in Burundi, I was unable to run to purchasing a white metal bath, so got the local stonemason to make me one using cement blocks on top of which were applied smooth, thin, sloping layers of cement, with a waste-pipe and plug incorporated into the base of the bath.

John, fired by a pioneer missionary-spirit, caught the vision and set about supervising a very skilled Ugandan stonemason in making a much more superior version. He made it standard bath size and shape, inside and out, again with outlet and plug, and the result, after putting layer-upon-layer of thin cement, day-after-day (previously sifted through my flour sieve!), was a cement bath whose smoothness defied any metal competitor. John had thought his DIY days had come to a happy end after four years in the UK, but he soon discovered that he had really only just begun! In God's economy, *nothing* is ever wasted!

John suggested to his pastor-friend that he and his wife, plus the two of us, would do well to have a day of prayer and fasting to seek the Lord's mind about our spiritual work. The man looked somewhat taken aback and uncomfortable, but really had no legitimate reason, outwardly, to refuse. So a day was set. His wife was exceedingly unfit and, although she joined us for part of the morning prayer and we laid hands on her for healing, she could not be expected to fast, as such. She was in the early stages of pregnancy, having a recent history of miscarriages following a nasty fall in the kitchen, when she fell off a cupboard-top on to an upturned chair. Her husband seemed both unaware of, and unconcerned about, her condition.

This pastor-friend knew that I discerned something was wrong and, after that day of prayer and fasting, and further church-visiting, ongoing supervision of the work on the house, etc, we called at his home one morning early in November and discovered that his motorbike (a gift from some undiscerning spiritual organisation in the USA) was not, according to him, working at all, hence our finding him at home at that time of day.

It was the practice of most of the local 'pastors' to descend on the Post Office around ten o'clock in the morning, and in the lunch-hour, and for them all to stand outside the private post-boxes, where addressees' mail was placed ready for their collection, waiting for gift-cheques to arrive in the post from North America, from unsuspecting donors. Had one had a cine-camera, these pastors would have looked as if they were runners, standing at the starting-line, waiting for the whistle to blow, post-box keys at the ready to swoop on the booty!

While we were there, the Post Office sorting clerk was working a month's notice for accepting bribes from these local 'pastors' in order to put airmail envelopes with North American stamps affixed, addressed to another 'pastor', into *their* personal boxes so that they could pay the gift-cheques into their own bank accounts before the rightful owner had a chance to get his hands on them. The CID would often be called to split up street-fights between 'pastors' who had resorted to a public display of fisticuffs in order to determine who would gain credit from such gift-cheques. It was a question of the survival of the fittest. We saw none we would have deemed to be spiritually fit and, in any case, see grave dangers in pouring into unproven spiritual-work vast and regular sums of overseas' cash.

We had called that November morning, after much prayer, lovingly to challenge our pastor-friend, desirous of seeing him respond and sincerely repent, to effect changes in his life. He feigned quite convincing repentance, even with tears, for having spun us a yarn while we were still in England, by correspondence, telling us that he was savagely arrested at the

150

Ugandan border, and of the torture which was supposedly meted out to him, in the hope that we would take pity and, like his naïve American supporters, send him a handout. He agreed that he had made the story up, because his incredulous wife knew it was a complete fabrication, and he was forced to deny these events to save face with her.

Soon after our arrival at his house, he had pleaded with John not to confront him saying, "It will only cause problems in my marriage," thereby acknowledging that things were wrong. His wife graciously forgave this particular sin, but none of us knew that day just how many more were to come to the surface within a short space of time.

Very unusually, I found myself driving, around 1.30 p.m. that same day, to the Post Office as we were expecting some urgent mail. Who should be driving in the opposite direction, back home from the Post Office, but our pastor-friend, on the *very motorbike* he had told us was "not working *at all*", and which was, in fact, in perfect working-order! I began to see that he had lied to us yet again in order to get money out of us, although we rarely complied with his hopes. However, when I stuck my hand out of the car-window and waved to him, at once he turned his head the other way, ignored me, our car and my wave, and drove at top speed on the other side of the road. There were very few cars at all in that town, and our Subaru Estate, with its red bodywork and white roof, was unique almost anywhere in Kenya, let alone in that small town.

I was sure that the Lord had brought me at this unusual time of day in order to manifest something to us that we needed to know. Having picked up the mail out of our post box, I drove straight home and recounted the events of the last ten minutes

151

to John. He agreed at once that they were significant. We asked the Lord to confirm our suspicions that something much more serious was afoot, and He did within three days.

We received various visitors in a stream, who knew our friend well, and each came to 'warn us', somewhat belatedly, but typically, because of initial lack of moral courage, that our friend had taken two other common-law wives and had children by both of them, and was also regularly sleeping around with the town's prostitutes and drinking locally-brewed gin, which is exceptionally potent. When he had received John's letter from England earlier, accepting his invitation to be a co-pastor of his imagined eight new churches (which he had actually coerced other church leaders into allowing him to take over, with the false promises of material handouts from the 'new missionaries' who were coming), he temporarily ditched his other wives and women, straightened out his life somewhat *on the surface*, went back to his first, lawful wife and lived with her at home. Therefore, by the time we pitched up, everything in the garden *looked* as if it had always been rosy to anyone without spiritual insight, which by now he very much hoped I had lost! In fact, his invitation to John never included *me* at all!

Apparently a couple of years earlier he had beguiled two American visitors by 'hiring' a stone-built church from a more 'successful' pastor for the two weeks of their visit, taking over the church, choir, elders and members, while he put on a convincing act as 'Pastor'. The 'rent' for the church, payable to the real pastor, was agreed to be half of the regular, monthly gift-cheques our friend would receive from the States! All were most happy to comply, and the trick worked ... until a third, jealous pastor wrote to the donors and spilt the beans, in the hope that *he* himself would be sent the gift-cheques instead as an eminently suitable alternative, in his eyes!

The whole background to this area needs to be understood. A man called Elijah Masinde formed a cult in 1943 called 'Dini ya Msambwa' (the religion of the ancestors or ancestral spirits) which was banned by the Kenya Government in 1976. Masinde taught his followers, who considered him to be '*the* Messiah', to hate Europeans and to refuse to wear western-style clothes and instead dress in monkey-skins, while hypocritically posing for his portrait-photograph wearing a topee and collared-shirt and tie! He claimed the power to heal the deaf, blind and crippled. The cult practised polygamy, he himself having five wives and twenty nine children, plus grandchildren. Followers believed Masinde to be a prophet sent by God to save Africans from foreign religions. They did not accept Jesus as the Saviour of the world, but only of white races. Masinde had a very large following, not only from the whole of East Africa, but from other African countries as well, making a total of possibly fifty thousand members of this cult. Although banned, secret meetings continued to be held, especially in the very town and district where we had gone to live and work.

Many principalities and powers behind this cult have not yet been dethroned in spiritual battle, as far as we are aware. It would take a strong team of mature, righteous Christian leaders, during a prolonged time of prayer and fasting, to topple these satanic influences.

If only our informers had had the pluck to come and warn us *before* we had gone to all the trouble and expense of moving all the way from the capital to Western Province, leaving Paul behind with guardians, and generally upsetting our family life. But the Lord *had* sought to speak to us through my own lack of peace - His most usual way of warning us that something is wrong, and asking us to wait at His red light, before we moved forward.

We knew what we had to do! First, we repented of being disobedient and going determinedly through the only visible open door, and asked the Lord to re-direct our steps very clearly. We then gave notice at once on the house we were living in, with workmen still having not quite finished externally, all of which proved an enormous strain. We had advanced so much cash in workmen's wages and building-materials that we now needed to live in the house rent-free for the best part of another three months to recoup the value.

Paul's Christmas school-holidays were due to begin shortly after this, so we left the animals in charge of two lady-helpers we had taken on earlier to assist with house-work and digging the field that was meant to be our front-garden while we spent a couple of weeks in Nairobi finding an alternative home. We then collected Paul to bring him to Western Province for the Christmas holidays. Julia came too for a week's youth camp organised by her mission at the local school.

The very day after we had returned to Nairobi to house-hunt once more, the Lord performed a lovely miracle. Of all places, we were in a pet shop purchasing a choke-chain for Rex when I suddenly looked at the customer ahead of us. He was wearing a 'kippah' (Jewish prayer-cap) and excitedly I nudged John's arm, but he, too, had noticed. We got our purchase hastily out of the way, and quickened our footsteps to catch up with our departing Jewish friend. I greeted him with, "Shalom!" and he responded warmly. We told him we had recently visited

Israel and he beamed, telling us that he was both a Sabra (native-born Israeli) and the Minister of the Nairobi Synagogue, no less! (He was not yet a full rabbi.)

As we got outside it was raining, so he graciously invited us into his parked car in order to exchange backgrounds and addresses. It was, through this intervention of God, that He was now reminding us of our first, real priority for His work, namely to be involved in a prayer-work for the Jewish people. This would mean seeking His opportunities of educating Kenyan Christians concerning our debt to Israel and encouraging those whom He had called to pray both privately and in groups for the Jews. In addition, it would be essential to go to the Synagogue fairly regularly in order to demonstrate active love to the Hebrew Congregation in Nairobi, numbering some one hundred and twenty Jewish families. This was *His* open door, and one we walked through thereafter. Also we needed to be in Nairobi, both for Paul's schooling and to fulfil our Jewish-based ministries, which could not possibly fit with Western Province! How merciful and timely are the Lord's acts and how patiently He draws us back when we have followed what seemed a good idea instead of His *perfect* plan.

We found a new home quite quickly through Paul's guardians' church, as one of their elders had built a new house on his large plot, was moving out of the old one into the new, and agreed that we could rent his former house for quite a reasonable rent. This house was in Karen, the residential area adjoining Langata where Paul's day-school was situated.

It was a large, spacious house, built in a mixture of timber and stone, with five bedrooms and set in three acres of land, mainly fenced off for cattle-grazing. We were very thankful

155

to the Lord for this provision, and the landlord promised he would have the house redecorated, with all wooden floors in reception rooms duly sanded and polyurethaned, early in the New Year, 1984, ready for our moving in.

It was going to be hard to go back to Western Province, even temporarily, as our hearts were just not there at all, especially after the opening the Lord had given us with the Minister of the Synagogue in Nairobi. But return we did, with Paul and Julia, to begin repacking *yet again!* Somehow, however, we had to provide twelve-year-old Paul with some holiday distraction, missing Louise's company as he was, and try to celebrate Christmas amidst the packing-cases!

One redeeming feature was that we lived near to the local airstrip, where we were in the habit of taking Rex for his evening constitutional. Paul looked forward to going for this walk each day after tea, and I had bought him a football for Christmas, which he was then able to kick around on the barely-used tarmac airstrip.

We taught Rex to run after and return sticks, and tried to discipline him to obey certain instructions such as, "Heel!" etc. As he was already fifteen months old, our success was somewhat limited, but we made a start. What was not so easy was trying to dissuade him that the local poultry-population was not there for his sole benefit to run after and kill. He was walking quite sedately to heel one evening when suddenly he spotted a hen on the verge before we did. He was not leashed at the time, and took one flying leap at the clucking chicken. John went after him, with Paul bringing up the rear, and they just managed to retrieve him in time, but it took all the self-control we could muster not to laugh as he emerged with bunches of feathers

156

sticking out of either side of his mouth and clinging to his wet nose, looking for all the world like a walrus!

The local population was petrified of Rex, and children would scream if he came within twenty yards of them. This had its advantages, as it prevented people, in general, from helping themselves gratis to our domestic water-supplies from an outside-tap. John had set up a running-wire around one side of the house, with a large metal hoop and long dog-chain, so that Rex could exercise freely whether we were in or not. This enabled him successfully to guard the property day and night into the bargain.

We discovered that the Sugar Company, some thirty miles away, ran a social club that had a beautiful swimming pool and we were given special permission to use it whenever we wished. At only four thousand or so feet above sea-level, the climate was usually very warm and humid, so it was ideal weather for Paul to go swimming whenever we could make it. Sometimes I left John to take him to the pool while I stayed behind to get packing, cooking or correspondence completed.

On Christmas Day we attended Morning Service at the local Anglican church, had lunch at the hotel and then spent the afternoon with the Baptist family who lived next door to our ex-pastor-friend, the latter having backslidden totally into every conceivable kind of sin, and having left his lawful wife to live with his second and third wives in rotation.

Our Baptist friends were a unique family and, despite their twelve children and various relatives coming and going, the household was peaceful and the whole family well-disciplined. The parents had held rehearsal sessions with their younger fry in order to practise singing songs to entertain their missionary-guests. The Abaluhya tribes of Western Province are well known for their musical ability, as are many other pure Bantu tribes, and the children did us and their parents proud as they sang carols and choruses, much to our delight. They were a veritable little choir! Their father was the local photographer who had his own town-studio, so we had, of course, to have our photograph taken in their garden with the whole family present that afternoon.

Prior to leaving Western Province for good, we had begun housegroup meetings for Bible study and prayer, starting in our own house and then moving to a neighbour's home once we had reached the point of eliminating our possessions in order to move to Nairobi. This neighbour generously gave us a live chicken as his Christmas gift to us, so we killed it and prepared it for the pressure-cooker, along with vegetables, for our Boxing Day lunch. This time Rex did not offer his assistance in slaughtering the fowl!

The New Year was upon us before we could turn round. We were forced often to eat lunch at the hotel because by this time we had had to pack all our cooking-utensils. We arranged for the local bus company to collect and deliver our effects by lorry to Karen but, in fact, we arrived at our new home by car long before they did.

17. Let My People Go (Ex. 5:1)

We could hardly believe, on arriving at our house in Karen, that we could not move in that day, as arranged. This was becoming a *habit!*

There were the landlord, his wife and teenage children, on all fours, applying polyurethane varnish to the newly-sanded sitting-room floor (which was the size of a small church-hall) while the hired sander whirred all around them in adjacent rooms with wooden floors, creating clouds of dust everywhere, including over the sticky, newly-varnished floor! The whole place looked and smelt like a timber mill!

There was absolutely no way that we could enter, let alone move in, and the floors remained wet for at least the next couple of days. We began to wonder whether any prospective landlord ever took would-be tenants seriously when they agreed they would definitely move in on a certain day. Yes, they wanted the rent in advance - no doubt about that at all - but to have the property ready when *actually* needed, that was another story!

There are two quite separate modes of time-keeping in Africa: local and European time. It seems almost hypocritical to announce that a church meeting is due to begin at 2 p.m. when one knows perfectly well one actually means between 3 and 4 p.m. to allow everyone time to arrive late! Or, if it is raining, not at all! And 'tomorrow' can usually mean anything up to a week's time. It is quite common for preachers and elders to wander into church services half-way through, and even more usual for preachers to arrive on platforms totally unprepared to preach, but managing to waffle on for at least an hour! No wonder the

159

members tend to be spiritually dry in many cases, and do not hurry to get themselves to church on time.

Our new landlord kindly housed us in the guest-room of his new house, containing three beds, for a couple of nights while the varnish dried out in our own house. We had to giggle as we tried to hang up our clothes in the guest-room wardrobe, as the hanging-rail was almost at ceiling level and was clearly only made for giraffes!

Eventually, with the floor finally dry, we could live in our own home, start unpacking essentials and begin to have a more settled existence once more.

Paul was so obviously relieved to be living under the same roof as his parents. We had all missed each other, not least he and I! He enjoyed the large garden and the company of the landlord's sons. Within days of moving, he had to resume school, but began noticeably at once to make academic-progress now that he was back with us. He had been very happy with his guardian-family, who had shown him much love and kindness, but he missed his own family and all that that meant.

Three months after moving into this particular house and worshipping at the same church as Paul's former guardians, the opportunity arose for me to speak on the subject of Exodus II. Attached to this church was a Tuesday morning ladies' Bible study, which I attended regularly, and two of its members kindly agreed to make a 'Let My People Go' banner for the evening talk I was to give. They made a superb job of it, and I was very thrilled with their efforts. The husband of Paul's former guardian-couple, who was an engineer, graciously offered to draw a map of Eastern Europe depicting the main exit routes which Steve Lightle had had revealed to him ten years earlier while in West Germany.

I contacted a young Kenyan pastor who was musically gifted and he agreed to train a choir for the occasion, while our church ladies' guild offered to provide refreshments for the end of the meeting.

While preparing myself to give this talk I received a tune, with words, from the Holy Spirit on this same theme and our musical pastor-friend agreed to sing this solo during the meeting.

We invited members of the Hebrew congregation to join us, and one plucked up courage to do so, and he also purchased a copy of the book, 'Exodus II'. The turn-out for the meeting was not terribly large, but quite a number of people from the church attended with some outside folk besides. It was an honour to have one Jew present, at any rate, and he was quite a key person in the Hebrew Community.

Doubtless, some of the audience thought I was stark, staring bonkers, but I am used to that! And a beginning had been made to be obedient to the Lord's clear calling to share with at least a part of the Body of Christ what our responsibility is to the Jewish people, and to inform them about Exodus II. They listened with rapt attention to the message, and it obviously gave some of them food for thought.

We trusted the Lord to enable us to visit Israel again that same year (1984), and to attend the Christian Feast of Tabernacles' celebration. In our church was a single lady called Marylyn and, not only did she show special interest in accompanying us, looking as she was for somewhere to go on holiday, but the Lord immediately burdened her to join us each week to intercede for Israel and His ancient people, thus becoming not only a prayer-partner but a close friend also.

A few months before we were due to go to the Feast, the Synagogue Minister had a visit from a rather strange character who told him he had had a dream where he saw himself in Israel among a large number of people. The minister referred this Kenyan man to us, to test whether we found him as peculiar as he did! This man discovered we were going to Israel the following September and decided, willy nilly, that he was coming also, although we never invited him.

It was all rather disastrous, as we found him to be a false prophet who was to try repeatedly to divide the group, setting one against another, as the mood took him. He was a supposed freelance-evangelist, but his main interest in going to Israel was to try to sell music cassettes his own Kenyan choir had recorded. He told us that, before he became a Christian (and we never had real proof that he was born again) he was a nightclub singer.

We visited his home before the trip and discovered he had a very sweet, well-educated, teacher-wife who was genuinely spiritual. It was suggested we have a time of prayer, when she prayed very much to the point and in agreement with scripture. We also prayed in turn, but we had scarcely begun when suddenly, he noisily bolted out of the door and remained outside until we had finished. His behaviour was very far from that of the evangelist he had said he was.

We also met him in town on a few occasions in the lunch-hour to help him tie up loose administrative ends in preparing for his trip. We ate and prayed inside our car, parked in a quiet spot near a large park. Naturally, we had taken picnic-style food with us to eat cold, mostly consisting of quiches, of

162

which he was both critical, and always returned an unfinished portion, with his nose turned up in disgust! "I am defeated with *your* cold food!" he exclaimed, "I have tried, but I don't like it. It is not what we are used to eating!"

The second time this sort of thing happened, I felt it was time for me to respond. "Well, if you have decided that the Lord wants you to travel overseas, including Israel, perhaps you should begin asking Him for grace both to like and eat cold food, because the Israelis eat salad breakfasts *every* morning in the summer months, and you may cause offence if you return food uneaten, to say nothing of going hungry!"

Quite undeterred, he changed the subject rapidly to finance. There was never an occasion when we were to meet that he did not ask the same question repeatedly, "How much will going to Israel cost?" We had sent him full figures in writing, and explained again and again by telephone, when we saw him in town, visited his house, and even on the eve of our departure, when he stayed the night at our house, by which time it was far too late to add or subtract any foreign exchange, for which he had long ago sought and obtained Central Bank permission.

To fly direct to Israel and spend several weeks there proved too expensive, so we found a cheaper route via Cairo, Egypt. So our 'evangelist', Marylyn, John and I boarded a flight from Nairobi to Cairo and, after a smooth passage, arrived in the Turkish-bath atmosphere of Cairo. We hired a taxi and had the most awful journey to a downtown hotel. The driver deliberately tried to bang a rival cabby with the bumper of his brand new car and, like everyone else on the road, honked his horn incessantly, while he thought nothing of driving down the

163

wrong side of the road! It was hair-raising to say the least. Marylyn and I sat in the back praying silently, although at one stage I threatened to get out if he did not desist. By some miracle we arrived in one piece at the hotel.

We seemed to spend our time perpetually haggling over prices and never reaching an amicable agreement. Egyptians seem to change their minds every half-second when it comes to prices and it was a relief, after two days, to be leaving Cairo.

On the eve of our departure from the hotel we arranged with Reception to eat breakfast the next morning very early in order to be at the bus-terminal no later than 06.45, and asked them kindly to arrange a suitable taxi for us. When we reached the dining-room all was in complete darkness, with not a single member of staff in sight. We reported to Reception and found sundry Egyptians all lolling around, and the staff were adamant that they would *not* serve breakfast until we had not only paid the bill in full which, of course, we had every intention of doing before our departure, but at what was rapidly becoming the typically augmented-rate, which we dreaded, since our currency was inevitably very limited.

We had long discussions with the 'lollers' (who turned out to be taxi-driver friends of the hotel-management, all of whom were vying for our custom at exorbitant prices) and, eventually, with hardly any time to spare, the hotel deigned to give us breakfast, accepted a compromise-settlement of the bill somewhere between the original agreed price and a fraction of the new, higher one, and out we all rushed, thankful to be released. Yet only to get involved in still another of the same ilk with the taxi-driver who differed as to where he decided we

164

should go, plus the no-longer-novel changing of his mind as to the taxi-fare he wanted us to pay.

By some divine intervention we managed to find the right bus and get ourselves and our luggage on board just in time. The bus was a brand new, air-conditioned one with superbly comfortable seating but, so new was it that the air-conditioning had not been tested and adjusted, and we nearly froze all the way to the Egyptian-Israeli border where one changes buses. This was in sharp contrast to the searing temperatures we had encountered in Cairo by day.

The bus journey was absolutely fascinating, driving as we did, on a good, tarmac road, through Goshen, and being told the area had barely changed since the time of Moses. Then we boarded a ferry to cross the Suez Canal, which I had last seen in 1965 when I sailed on a passenger-ship from London to Mombasa, en route for Burundi, with my missionary-colleague and friend, Marguerite.

Three out of the four of us had raging headaches the whole time we were in Egypt, yet pain-killers did nothing. However, the second we crossed over into the Promised Land, *all* headaches lifted simultaneously! It was as if our Great Physician were now on a local call, as opposed to a trunk one. How much we rejoiced that we had come 'up from Egypt', and this brought fresh revelation as to how the children of Israel must have felt in the first Exodus. What a contrast from Cairo, full as it was with smells and 'hells' of oppression and gross poverty, leading to inevitable extortion, particularly of tourists, and constant, tiring and tiresome bartering. Yet it was well worth the experience, and brought Moses' book of Exodus alive.

Our evangelist-companion did not seem to be quite with us each time we prayed, and it was all very reminiscent of the time we had tried to pray with him in his house, and there was something about him that was curiously similar to our ex-'pastor'-friend with whom we had worked in Western Province. But on one thing we were all in total agreement: never, but never again, would we return to Egypt. Enough was more than enough! Praise God that He is doing a continuing work of salvation, however, in the lives of numerous Egyptians. The prophet Isaiah said, "In that day shall Israel be third with Egypt and with Assyria, even a blessing in the midst of the land: Whom the Lord of hosts shall bless, saying, "Blessed be Egypt My people, and Assyria the work of My hands, and Israel Mine inheritance." (Isaiah 19:24-25) The old enemies of Israel will ultimately unite in a common faith in Almighty God with His blessing.

18. The Feasts of the Lord (Leviticus 23:2)

The bus reached Jerusalem in record time as it was the eve of *Rosh HaShanah* (Jewish New Year) and the driver was keen to be home well before evening when the Feast Day begins officially, all Jewish days starting and ending at dusk.

Rosh HaShanah is not a biblical festival. Originally it was observed in Spring on First Nisan (Ex. 12:2), but it is celebrated on the first day of the month of *Tishri*, during our September or October, and it is the first of the High Holy Days, the Ten Days of Repentance, which usher in *Yom Kippur*, The Day of Atonement, on tenth *Tishri*. *Rosh HaShanah* is heralded with the sounding of the *shofar* (ram's horn), as related in Leviticus 23:23-25, proclaiming God's sovereignty (Ps. 98:6); it reminds man of his responsibility to keep God's commandments (Ex. 19:16) and it warns against impending judgment (Amos 3:6). It will be such a *shofar* which announces the approaching *great day of the Lord* (Zeph. 1:14-16) and welcomes Messiah's coming (Is. 27:13) The traditional greeting of '*L'Shanah Tovah Tikatayvu*' ("May you be inscribed for a good year!") is passed between Jew and Jew the world over, believing, as they do, that repentance to God for their sins will ensure that they are written in His book of life.

The Day of Atonement is kept as a solemn day of total fasting and prayer and there are meetings in the synagogues, some lasting many hours. We felt that we wanted to observe this in a similar way and invited Marylyn and our evangelist-companion to join us in our hotel bedroom where we could pray undisturbed.

167

John began by reading to us Leviticus 23 to remind us of this day's origins. Our friend appeared not to be feeling very comfortable or happy, slammed and zipped up his Bible even before we had finished reading, and announced he was going to his room. John asked him if he would be long, and he replied, "No, I am *just* going!" He *just* went indeed. He returned to his bedroom and slept for the whole day, refusing to join us or pray with us! He had seemed quite unable even to pray with us back in Kenya, especially with his wife present, and here we were again with the same situation repeating itself.

We were gravely disappointed, but not entirely surprised. From that day on he asked the Arab management in our hotel at Abu Dis (Bethany) to move him to the floor above, "away from *those* people," and refused to greet or talk to us at all, or share a meal-table with any of us. The hotel-staff became exasperated with him as he would go and knock one of them up from the staff-bedrooms at dawn in order to prepare his breakfast, without prior warning, or, on the other hand, he would pitch up extremely late for meals he had ordered at a certain time, and then leave them untouched.

Many of the hot meals were prepared by the Proprietor's sister-in-law, who was an excellent cook, whose husband drove the food by car from the next village where they lived. It was not, therefore, very convenient or easy to keep it warm and fresh, and the almost empty hotel did not employ a resident cook or kitchen-hand, as such. Various relatives shared the work, including a very sweet school-age boy called Zakaria, who seemed both willing and able to cope with the whole range of duties from manning Reception to cleaning, laundering, serving

168

food, and pouring drinks from the bar, the latter appearing to bring in a fair amount of regular trade from local Arabs.

We spent three and a half weeks in Israel, mainly in Jerusalem, attending the Feast of Tabernacles, or *Succot*, which begins on 15th *Tishri*. *Succot* is related both to the beginning of Israel's nationhood and to the agricultural year. It is also called the *Feast of Ingathering* (Ex. 23:16) because by the autumn all the fruits of the earth have been gathered and the harvest garnered.

Succot is very much a season of rejoicing (Lev. 23:40 and Deut. 16:14), not only because the harvests are safely gathered in but because it follows the Day of Atonement, with its assurances that God's people have been cleansed by the atoning blood of the lamb.

As one goes about Jerusalem, or for that matter other Jewish quarters of Israel, one can see booths or tabernacles constructed of olive, pine, myrtle and other tree branches (Lev. 23:40 and Neh. 8:14-16) built on rooftops, balconies, in gardens and courtyards. It is essential to build a flimsy, temporary dwelling, through which one can see the heavens, to remind God's ancient people of their time of tabernacling in the wilderness of Egypt, while praying the weather will not be wet!

Marylyn, a mezzo-soprano, was invited to sing in the Feast of Tabernacles' Choir and she had to attend many rehearsals lasting long hours, but despite her comparatively late arrival in Jerusalem, some time after most other singers had begun rehearsing, she fitted in perfectly and caught up within a very short season.

In a sense, Marylyn was a kind of 'first-fruits' for us, not only in catching our own vision for intercession for the Jewish people and Exodus II, but in actually going to Israel to comfort

Zion. Very wonderfully the Lord opened a door later for her to serve Him, with all her gifts and skills, spiritual and practical, in the heart of Jerusalem and, miss her greatly though we did, especially as a friend and prayer-partner, we rejoiced that He had her where He desired her to be at that time, and therein she was fulfilled.

We came, frankly, to dread and dislike any so-called 'holy site' in Israel, and found such places had a distinct oppression about them. Marylyn and I discovered that we were affected identically and spontaneously by these sites without prior verbal reference between us. When, for example, we visited the Church of the Nativity in Bethlehem, which is Jesus' supposed birthplace, with queues of people mostly from Continental Europe waiting first to enter the grotto, and then kneeling and kissing the flagstone marking the spot where Jesus is said to have been born, we felt claustrophobic at the very same moment, looked at each other and bolted for the exit as one! Perhaps rather irreligiously, we referred to such places thereafter as 'grotty grottoes'.

She did not know this at the time, but I felt exactly the same in 1983 when my Jewish ex-work colleague from London, Joan, with her husband, Avraham, had taken us to Nazareth to the Church of St Joseph, attributed to being the traditional site of Joseph's workshop, plus the Basilica of the Annunciation, incorporating the grotto where the Angel Gabriel is said to have told Mary she was to bring forth a Son and was to call Him Jesus (Luke 1:31).

My Jewish friend Joan, her husband, children, parents-in-law, brother-in-law and his family, had all made *aliyah* (returned to the land of their forefathers) many years earlier.

170

Every time we visited Israel, we were made extremely welcome by their whole, extended family in their homes on the outskirts of Tel Aviv. I believe that, *in God's economy*, He has His purposes in a friendship that has spanned fifty-plus years. Joan has shared with me that she finds orthodox synagogue-services 'a man's world', and feels that they are empty and dull for her, which I can understand when the women are segregated on an upstairs balcony, often behind a net curtain. I personally *love* synagogue, but then I attend as a believer in the One Who has torn the veil to the Holy of Holies asunder, once and for all. I see *His* fulfilment in God's Word and the *siddur* (prayer book).

Although it is not my calling to push Yeshua (Jesus) down the throats of the Jewish people, I long that many may come to a personal revelation of, and faith in, their Messiah and mine. It is amazing just how many Jews ask Christians the most searching questions and want to have precise and immediate answers! Some are even familiar with the New Testament as well as the Old, although the former is usually banned from being taught in schools. Yet others are Nicodemuses (secret believers) who remain within the security of the orthodox synagogues, or their own homes.

We have come to appreciate the Garden Tomb, in East Jerusalem, sited immediately above the Arab bus station. Most biblical sites come in pairs and, while the Garden may have its counterpart, for us it has always been very precious and real, and we personally believe, without a shadow of doubt, that it is *the* place of Jesus' burial and that the rock in the form of a skull outside the Garden, overlooking the bus station, so identifies with the biblical description of Golgotha that we sense it really *is* The Place of the Skull.

171

The whole area has such a Presence and peace that it has drawn hundreds upon hundreds of Christians over the years who wish to be quiet, hold services there and have gently conducted-tours by experienced Christians, free of charge, with no tourist-appeal as such. Those who staff the attached bookshop, and lead tour-parties, make no definite claim that the Garden is *The* Garden where Jesus was buried in the tomb of Joseph of Arimathea, as no one can ever be completely certain, but its history and geographical location certainly bear strong witness to this fact. Whenever we go to Jerusalem, we often rest, read, meditate and pray in that beautiful spot, whose atmosphere is in marked contrast to the noisy bus station below, and the souk (Arab market) inside the Damascus Gate of the Old City, a few minutes' walk away.

Prior to the Feast of Tabernacles' Christian celebration, we attended a Jerusalem-based messianic assembly, synagogues, the Baptist Church in Narkis Street and the Yad Vashem Holocaust Museum, where I was quite unashamedly weeping as I looked at photo after photo of holocaust-victims, before and after death, and visited other places of interest, mainly in the Old City. Whenever I have watched films on TV where victims are interviewed or visits are made to the concentration camps, it is as though I was there personally.

On that Yom Kippur in 1984 Marylyn was unmistakeably called to return to Jerusalem to serve the Lord Who underlined to her particularly Psalm 122:6, 'Pray for the peace of Jerusalem ...' and Psalm 137:5, 6, 'If I forget thee, O Jerusalem, let my right hand forget her cunning (or skill). If I do not remember thee, let my tongue cleave to the roof of my mouth; if I prefer not Jerusalem above my chief joy'. Hers was

172

not simply a call to just anything, anywhere in Israel. It was specifically to use her physiotherapy skills (performed very largely with her right hand) *in* Jerusalem.

The Feast was a wonderful experience, with some Orthodox Jews in attendance, and some Jewish speakers, including Jerusalem's then Mayor, Teddy Kollek. The Davidic worship, music, singing and dance and the costumes worn by performers were all outstandingly beautiful and everything enacted to an exceedingly high standard, bringing glory to the Lord. The messages given at the Feast, in both the general evening-sessions and optional daytime-seminars, were very deep and challenging, and many people were saved, filled with the Holy Spirit and healed.

Marylyn joined us one evening in going to the late Dr Derek Prince's healing meeting in the King David Hotel, where the meeting-hall was filled to overflowing on a hot, sultry evening which was rather trying due to lack of air-conditioning, in contrast to the Binyanei Ha'uma Convention Hall, where all the main evening-meetings were staged. However, one was able to forget about any discomfort as one watched the Lord miraculously heal so very many people.

Derek and his wife, Ruth, ministered to many themselves for several hours, but they also commissioned two Jewish messianic believer-couples to assist them, and the Lord never once drew any distinctions. Irrespective of who ministered, *He* was present to bless and heal.

If anything could spoil the Feast at all, it was the ongoing awkwardness and standoffishness of our friend whose attitude, despite the challenging messages, remained the same, if not worse.

One night we came in very late from one of the evening-sessions. He walked through the hotel-entrance and immediately commandeered one of the lady resident-guests, telling her to bring him tea and bread and put it on the coffee-table on the landing outside his bedroom-door!

By now it was nearly midnight, the guest was in the middle of watching a late-night TV film, and we were very embarrassed. As our friend was part of our group, albeit uninvited, we shared lovingly with him that it was not usual to ask fellow-guests to wait on us, especially so late at night, but that if he ordered extra food and drink it would be billed to him as 'extras'. That fixed it! The next morning we discovered the tray still on the table totally untouched. He had reasoned that, if he did not actually consume the food and drink, despite ordering it, he would not have to pay for it! Quite what he expected the hotel to do with cold tea, sour milk and stale bread we did not know!

The challenge not to request guests to serve him worked, but we had not bargained on his asking the hotel-proprietor himself. Once more we came in rather late and, as we passed the TV room, he shouted to the proprietor, "Bring me tea!" He graciously complied, adding it to the man's bill, but asked us the following morning if such behaviour was normal in Kenya. We hastened to reassure him, and apologised profusely, but the staff did not seem convinced by his ongoing rudeness and bad manners. While our friend's wife was educated, her husband was not. He was brash and proud, refusing all advice and help, even before we left Kenya. We feared his conduct would cause offence to Arabs and Jews, both of whom have codes of ethics which they observe to the letter.

Our friend ran out of cash by the time we were due to leave Jerusalem to move on to Mount Carmel for a week, and finally to the Tel Aviv area to prepare for our departure. He had taken more than sufficient money for his food, bus fares, etc., but had squandered both time and money going around as many music-studios as he could discover, in the hope of selling his Kenyan choir's music-cassettes to them, and even trying to persuade some innocent soul to sponsor a visit to Israel by his group. As far as we know, he went on trying, and we believe the Lord will keep the door firmly shut because of his hypocrisy, unless he is able to repent.

We moved, together with Marylyn, to the Stella Carmel Christian Guest-House on Mount Carmel, and had a very different kind of stay there, but a most enjoyable and restful one. The staff were extremely kind. We arrived on a Friday afternoon to find the place full of guests and messianic believers who had gathered for an Erev Shabbat celebration (Sabbath Eve meal, with prayers). It was wonderful to be part of such company with believers' whole families present for the joyous occasion.

After getting up one morning at Stella Carmel, I was trying to open a stiff bedroom sash-window which had a writing-desk in front of it. Something seemed to click at the base of my spine, and I became rigid, with a trapped-nerve affecting the circulation in my right leg. As a skilled physiotherapist, Marylyn set about massaging my back regularly, and 'pegged me out' - that is to say, I would lie flat on my back on my bed and she would gently put her cupped hands under my chin and stretch my body to release the pressure on the sciatic-nerve.

One of the Stella Carmel senior staff prayed for my healing, and it was some time later that we began to realise there

175

was a spiritual link between our uninvited evangelist-companion, whom we had left behind in Jerusalem to make his own way back to Cairo a week before our own departure was due, and this back-trouble, which I had never had before.

He had tried constantly to stir up strife and division between John and me, or Marylyn and one of us, and was highly critical of us all, complaining that good manners were 'just European'. We forgave him at once for all his negative actions and attitudes, as each occurred.

Jerusalem is well known in Christian circles for its spirits of division and infirmity. It seemed he had managed successfully to cause both to be manifested and, as has been explained previously, it is very common for curses to be put on one through such resentment, bitterness and strife.

While at Stella Carmel we visited Haifa, Israel's main port, and Akko (Acre), the former being a deep-water port. Akko was known as Ptolemais during Paul's lifetime, being only briefly mentioned in the New Testament. It became the Crusaders' kingdom, following the capture of Jerusalem by the Saracens. I was very aware of spiritual oppression in this place, and did not really enjoy our visit there, conscious as I am that the Crusaders performed a holocaust upon the Jews, calling them 'Christ-killers' and believing that they were doing God a favour in silencing them once and for all.

From Stella Carmel we went on to Yaffa (Joppa) for three nights in order to be near Tel Aviv where we were due to catch our bus back to Cairo Airport. At Yaffa we stayed at a Messianic hostel and the October weather was still sufficiently warm by day for us to eat our meals out-of-doors, as is the hostel's tradition in spring and summer months. The shops were

176

full of tempting displays of dried fruit and nuts which, while not cheap, are of top quality, so we stocked up before our departure. But dried fruit was one of John's weaknesses, and he could never resist stealing the odd sultana or raisin when I was making fruit cakes or puddings at home. If we were to have any left at all with which to cook on our return, I had to hide the dried apricots, nuts and cake-fruit and pack it in my own luggage, so that he had no access to it.

It will be remembered that it was from Joppa that Jonah embarked on his voyage to Tarshish (Jonah 1:3). As we faced returning to Cairo, Jonah, one of my favourite biblical characters, had all our sympathy for wilfully boarding a ship going in the wrong direction. How we wished we could have flown back to Kenya from Tel Aviv instead!

While in Yaffa, we walked through a fairly new shopping-mall where we passed the door of what is renowned as the house of Simon the Tanner, where Peter had his vision on the rooftop (Acts 10:9-33). Additionally, of course, Yaffa is where Peter raised Tabitha from the dead (Acts 9:14).

Boarding the Cairo-bound bus from Tel Aviv, as opposed to Jerusalem, the journey took that much longer. This time, however, we had the benefit of a guide on board who was multi-lingual. There were several francophone Jewish passengers whom we presumed were visiting Israel and Egypt from France, as they did not look North African. Once again, my French came in useful!

Several events occurred during our long wait at the airport, happening, naturally, only to Marylyn and me - never to John! First of all, we paid a call to the Ladies', only to be met by an extremely smart young woman who looked more like an off-

177

duty air hostess than a washroom-attendant. Quite unabashed, she asked us for ten dollars *each* for the privilege of using the facilities! We had absolutely no money with us, and had parked our handbags with John, so could shrug our shoulders and quite honestly plead total poverty. After a long bus journey, we looked convincingly grubby and crumpled, anyway! Mercifully, when we were forced to return to the same rendezvous some hours later, our chic lady-attendant had disappeared and we had the place to ourselves.

Having several hours to kill, I decided it would be useful to check with a small air-charter company to see if they had a copy of their current timetable and tariff, lest anybody else from East Africa was crazy enough to fly to Israel via Cairo and wished to go on to Tel Aviv by air.

The office was up a narrow flight of concrete-stairs which was in complete darkness. We found the appropriate door, only to discover that the staff had already shut up shop. On our way down, a nasty-looking man suddenly shouted at us from the bottom of the steps in angry Arabic, gesticulating wildly up the dark stairway and presumably indicating that we had no business up there. He immediately blocked our path, but could not handle two of us at once against opposing walls of the passage, so Marylyn managed to slide past, leaving me in his clutches. We protested our genuine innocence in English, to no avail. He continued to holler abuse at me and got hold of the front of my blouse, much to my disgust. I have to confess to being terrified. Poor Marylyn did not know whether to keep going ahead or to return to give me support, but decided on the former, which proved to be wise as he probably suspected she would call for help, or possibly report him. He clearly thought we had been trespassing or spying, or both, yet we could not communicate. How thankful we were that neither of us had been on our own, but even more grateful that our Guardian Angel had been on duty!

Having got over that shock and returned safely to John, who was sitting on a bench guarding all the baggage in the main departure-terminal, Marylyn and I decided later on to go to see if we could go through Customs early and get rid of our various suitcases. We spotted a glass-fronted kiosk in the Customs' hall bearing the name of the airline we were to use, and went over to it. An efficient-looking uniformed lady was just about to enter. We appealed to her with our request. For a moment she looked pensive, only to advise us, "Here is what you do, ugh? You just wait until you are called, and then you just come through Customs with all the other passengers!" As this was at least another one and a half hours away, this did not help us in the slightest, and someone had to go on watching the luggage all the time, as ever was.

We were eventually called to the Customs' lounge where we had to sit and wait yet again. However, we were facing a window looking out onto an airport-entrance and, just prior to going through Customs, we were well entertained when suddenly an Egyptian dressed from head to foot in typical white, Islamic garb started arguing with another wearing a Kaffyah - a twisted, patterned turban. The man in white became increasingly irate and began lashing out with his tongue and fists at the man in the turban. A boxing-match had nothing on these two, and this scene had us enthralled, wondering who would win! Then, just as abruptly as the fight had started, of one accord they decided on a truce, smiled lovingly at each other and, locked in a

179

firm embrace, kissed each other's cheeks! Marylyn and I looked at each other, burst out laughing, and I coined the phrase: 'Rats-to-cats' to describe their totally contrasting facial expressions - one moment ratty and cross, and the next wearing Cheshire-cat grins from ear to ear. We have since realised this is all part of the Arab character.

What a relief it was to board the plane at last in the small hours of the morning. And it was even more blessed to return home to Kenya, met by Marylyn's super ex-Brigadier father, who drove us to our door. "Yes," the Brigadier agreed as we recounted all that had happened in Egypt, "the Egyptians are a funny lot! Quite unique really! They're not true Arabs, but somehow got washed down the Nile!"

19. They shall harass you in the land (Num. 33:55)

We were only able to enjoy our Karen home for fifteen months, with its nearby forest and two lovely dams, with much bird-life and even the occasional small buck visible.

Our next door European settler-neighbours in Karen were exceedingly uncooperative, with noisy dogs which provoked and fought constantly with our Alsatian, Rex, even through our bamboo-fence or double wooden-gates. The present landlord had originally purchased the entire plot from this family, on which their now rented house and ours were already built.

These unneighbourly neighbours comprised a middle-aged widow, her adult son plus live-in girlfriend. The schizophrenic son frequently went berserk, and behaved as if drugged. They were Kenya citizens of British background but their mode of life was unusually egocentric, and they were bent on being unreasonable toward us, possibly because we lived in what had initially been 'their' house, built by the late husband, and perhaps even more because we were Christians who brought some kind of silent challenge to their consciences. We sensed in them a whole host of principalities and powers which opposed everything we were and stood for.

We appealed to our Kenyan Christian landlord over the incessant barking of their pack of hounds, headed up by a mature, but brainless, Doberman, to which a younger one was added, with two remaining creatures of questionable pedigree, making four dogs in all. The tenants were frequently out on the town until late at night, whereupon the chief Doberman, and at

181

least one of the other dogs, would bark non-stop with a monotonous, metallic rasp until 'Ma' returned to put her 'Little Sweetie-Pies' to bye-byes in her bedroom! As she worked full-time by day, it does not take much to imagine the constant din he and the rest of the pack made most of the time.

Then suddenly, out of the blue, our landlord told us that he was giving both lots of tenants notice to quit and had, himself, had more than enough of barking-dogs. He went on to explain that he wanted to upgrade the two houses, modernise and redecorate, and re-let for double the rent! He knew we could not afford more than we were already paying for rent, and that he was safe in divulging this information. However, what he did *not* say was that he was moving us *out* of our house, moving the next-door neighbours *into* it, and finding new tenants for their vacant house!

We were shocked at his twisting the truth, for to move tenants from one house to another on the same plot is not giving them notice to quit, by any stretch of the imagination. Yet he told us frequently, face-to-face and over the telephone, that these neighbours were a thorough nuisance and he wanted them and their hounds out. Clearly he told them the same about us, only demonstrating once more the terrible hypocrisy practised even by church elders.

As far as we know, his desire to upgrade the dwellings and charge higher rents was probably true, yet he had not the moral courage to be specific as to his plans or the faith to trust the Lord for any shortfall our existing rent left, and our house was far from structurally sound, requiring John to do a lot of DIY on the roof, etc. In fact, we had a leak on the kitchen-verandah days before we were due to leave, so John went up on

182

the corrugated iron-roof to hammer a loose sheet back in place. In the middle of doing so, the landlord's wife sent her lady-gardener to ask us if we were intending to build because she could hear banging! I told the gardener to report to her boss that we would hardly be considering building on someone else's plot of land when we were preparing to move off it!

Our landlord had allowed us to use a broken fridge of his which we found already installed in our house when we first moved in. We spent some £75 having this repaired, with his approval. When we left he refused either to reimburse any of the repair-bill or, on the other hand, allow us to buy the fridge minus the cost of repairs, but instead used it himself in its renovated condition.

I began packing mechanically once again, wondering how many more times we must move house. There was no shortage of time for looking for a property as we had three months' notice, but the spiritual and emotional pressures from the landlord and the neighbours made us want to go as soon as ever possible, since both were in league to get us out.

One afternoon the neighbour's son got himself into a white-hot rage and let fly at John, who thought for a moment that he was going to hit him over the head! But the son managed to exercise sufficient self-control merely to utter the words, "You just get out of here. This is *my* place ...." Within days he and his mother had somehow gone to work on the landlord and got him to agree to fulfil the son's words (Proverbs 18:20-21).

The only house sufficiently close to Paul's school and anywhere large enough, at an affordable rent, was a shabby little single-storied, two-bedroomed guest-house, built on black-

183

cotton soil. It had a lean-to, corrugated iron-roof which John realised at once was not adequately sloped for rain run-off.

Roof-alterations, complete redecoration inside and out, and, wait for it …. polyurethane re-varnishing of the sitting-room parquet floor, had to be carried out before we could move in. Landlords never act in these areas until they are sure they have netted a new tenant. We agreed on the work needing to be done, the rent, and the moving-date. Another wile of landlords is to ask the would-be tenants what they consider needs repairing, painting, etc, in the hope that they will not notice too much, and find out the real state of the house after moving in, and get on and do it themselves, hopefully at their own expense!

Having done all but the last-minute packing, I offered to go over to the property and assist John with the building of a shed, there being neither garden-shed nor garage provided. It did not occur to me that sawing offcuts to predetermined lengths with an electric circular-saw would adversely affect my back, but the bending, and the particular angle at which I had to hold the saw while I cut some one hundred and fifty pieces of timber, did a lot of harm, and I found it hard to straighten up again.

We got the shed up amazingly fast, but I was to pay a high price in pain and discomfort, and this increased the 'pinched-nerve' sensation all the more in my right knee, and led to a lot of swelling.

Moving-Day dawned once more, and Christian friends came in minibuses and cars to help up transport our belongings, which we finished in a record couple of hours but … you've guessed it, the polyurethane varnish was *still* wet on the sitting-room floor, which was also the main-entrance to all other rooms, apart from the kitchen! This time, John decided to throw a plastic-sheet over the floor, wet varnish or no, and we marched over dry-shod. Thankfully all other floors were cement so they presented no problem, but it was at least a week before that wretched varnish would dry, but there was nothing for it but to leave the plastic in place.

I became deeply unhappy and unsettled in this house, yet we stuck it out for two years, during much of which we had little or no domestic water-supplies. I had to learn to recycle all laundry-water for the never-flushing toilet, and all dish-washing water, which we filtered through a double-layer of thick woven nylon, suspended over a couple of buckets by a wide elastic garter. We were forced to use this brew for watering passion fruit, lemon trees and the few flowers and shrubs we had in the minuscule garden.

The landlord had the most terrible house-helper we have ever had the misfortune to meet. She had a voice like a fog-horn, and would stand in her employer's back-yard, adjacent to our own house, and yell to the landlord's old mother, repeating several times a day the same news as to the latest gossip on each neighbour, including ourselves, as if we could not understand or hear. Much of what she had to say was malicious, back-biting rumour-mongering. She would speak in Swahili and the old lady would reply in Kikuyu, both understanding each other perfectly! Neither had enough to do, and what the house-helper was *supposed* to do she would rush around doing one hour before the landlord's wife returned home from her office each evening. It was always incredibly peaceful after 4 p.m.

We endured this for several months and then, because of the nature of her conversation day-by-day, we asked the Lord either to save her or remove her. He did the latter and shortly thereafter the old lady, having no other female with whom to gossip, departed for her up-country home, leaving the plot considerably quieter. Sadly, however, the male-farmhands took up where the house-help left off, and this was almost as difficult to bear.

Paul allowed me to use a small corner of his L-shaped bedroom as an office, and we began a lending-library of cassettes and books from or on the subject of Israel and the Jewish people, in order to promote intercession for them. We had a Messianic Jewish teacher-friend in Western Province who had been in Kenya for many years. She and another expatriate-teacher gave us the names and addresses of some of their own Christian contacts who had a prayer interest in Israel and they, in turn, gave us yet other names. Thereby we built up a mailing-list and, starting with the 1984 Feast of Tabernacles set of teaching-cassettes, plus others we already had and basic books such as Exodus II, a small beginning was made.

We also used Christian sources such as Prayer for Israel (UK) and Christian Friends of Israel (UK and Israel), and at one stage had over fifty folk on our mailing-list, some of whom met regularly together in small Area Meetings to intercede for Israel and the Jewish people in the Diaspora. Our vision was to see intercessors dotted all over Kenya, and even the rest of East Africa, with a God-given burden to pray for Israel and the Jews, and we counted ourselves very privileged to have a part in its fulfilment.

20. Let the Prophets Speak (I Cor. 14:29)

Most unexpectedly, the Lord provided for me to go to Israel and England in the Spring of 1986 in order to attend the Prophetic Word Ministries' (UK) Prophetic Gathering in Jerusalem during Easter week, and then briefly on to England to see relatives and friends, as I had not seen my parents and family for six years.

The Lord equally miraculously supplied the money for both John and Paul to attend the Gathering also, and John brought a small group of people with him from Kenya and Uganda.

I preceded the others by flying to Israel a week earlier and spending six days with Marylyn, who was by now living in West Jerusalem and was just completing her three months' *Ulpan* (intensive course in Hebrew). She was living with five other single ladies in a flat, so I made seven, and slept on one of the sofas in the living-room while Marylyn used the other.

The first night I was there I was awakened by what sounded like an African death-wail, and for a moment could not think where I was! One of the girls living in the flat had been born in the Caribbean, and I learnt the following morning that she was troubled frequently by nightmares which produced terrible fear and a wailing-sound, as if she had been suddenly bereaved.

Her cultural background was black African. After she had gone off to her temporary domestic job I asked Gail, the most senior flatmate, what the 'death-wail' had been all about during the night. Gail's reaction was electric! "*What* did you call

187

it?" she asked, seizing both my hands in hers. I repeated and explained what I meant. "Hallelujah, Oh, thank you, Jesus!" exclaimed Gail, "The Lord has brought you with the missing key! We have been asking Him to reveal the root of that dear girl's problem, and He has sent you from Africa with just the right experience to set her free!" And there was *I* thinking I had come for a week's holiday! But I have learnt that even, and especially when a Christian is 'on holiday', he is never on holiday from the Lord, Who Himself never slumbers nor sleeps, mercifully, and such times can be used by Him to put others in need across our paths.

Gail asked if I would join her in a day of prayer and fasting in order to minister to this young woman, who desperately wanted to be set free but had not known how. I was happy to agree, and Marylyn joined us for prayer during the morning-hours before going off to her afternoon choir-rehearsal for the Prophetic Gathering to be held the following week. Incidentally, it was marvellous to see Marylyn looking so well and happy, and being so fulfilled in the sphere of music in Israel.

The Lord gave us several words of knowledge, revealing a number of areas of bondage, all of which this girl confirmed that afternoon. She had prepared her heart for this time, but was understandably fearful of actual ministry, as many are, believing the devil's lie that he will so manifest his various brands of outburst, etc, thus preventing some from ever becoming free and getting even more deeply entrenched.

However, the Lord was so gentle with her as we quietly took authority over the spirits of death, etc, which had imprisoned her since childhood, and we cut her off spiritually in the name of Jesus from her entire background. She was

188

gloriously released and healed, and able to walk in total victory in the Christian life for the first time.

Interestingly enough, the Lord had already called that sister to serve Him in Kenya and she came the following year. Satan tried, after her arrival, to put those same old symptoms on her twice more, but she told him that he was a liar. Then, in place of symptom-nightmares (and I do stress that they were only symptoms, and that this is a common trick of the enemy to try to re-enter), the Lord Himself gave her a lovely dream. She saw her old house and beside it a high flight of steps. The Lord locked the door of the old house, led her up the steps and told her that He had sealed her past, led her away from it and that she was free from it forever. Hallelujah! 'Greater is He that is in us (believers) than he that is in the world' (Satan). (I Jn. 4:4).

In the interim, Gail had been roped in to sew the musicians' and dancers' costumes for the Gathering. Cash was at a premium, so garments from an earlier occasion were carefully unpicked, and I offered to help with pressing each piece of material to get out old stitching- and hem-lines, etc. We used vinegar-water and a cloth to press each one and, as a result, the entire flat smelt like a fish and chip shop for days!

Marylyn, Gail and I and took some time off to go down to the Dead Sea one day, and Marylyn and I went another day to visit a Jewish believer at Rehovot, for whom we had both been praying. That afternoon we travelled on by bus to Ashkelon on the Mediterranean coast as I had wanted specifically to pray on the spot over such a long-standing, local problem.

Gail was a very skilled seamstress and worked literal miracles in cutting, stitching and trimming beautiful costumes. No one could possibly have guessed that only a few days earlier

189

each new garment had been part of another costume from a previous performance. Is this not a parable of what the Lord does with our 'old nature' in 'giving us beauty for ashes, the oil of joy for mourning, the garment of praise for a spirit of heaviness, that we might be called trees of righteousness, the planting of the Lord, that He might be glorified'? (Is. 61:3 and Eph. 4:21-24).

I was sad to leave that happy abode on the Saturday evening, but was due to book into an Arab hotel in East Jerusalem in time for John, Paul and the East African group to join me in the hotel early the following morning, having flown overnight from Nairobi.

On the Sunday morning, bright and early, John breezed into the hotel bedroom to announce the flight had arrived ahead of schedule, and here they were! All had come primarily to attend the Easter Gathering in Jerusalem, with a few days tacked on either side for sightseeing.

Paul was extremely tired after the overnight-flight, and amazingly went to bed on arrival at the hotel 'for a brief rest' and had to be awakened that evening at suppertime. He could not think where he was as he looked bleary-eyed around his hotel bedroom, and assumed it was morning! He and daughter Louise have always had the gift of being able to sleep, without fuss, anywhere. I always used to tell Louise when she was younger that I was quite sure that she had the capacity to sleep on a clothes line, if necessary!

The opening session was the next evening, prior to which one had to go to the Binyanei Ha'uma conference hall in West Jerusalem, where the Gathering was to be held, to confirm one's registration. This enabled the East African group to have

190

most of Sunday and Monday to look around Jerusalem before the Gathering began.

Having had a hand in the costume pressing and been present when some of them were being stitched, I was doubly interested to see how they would look on stage. Merv and Merla Watson, from Canada, had worked really hard on singing and instrumentation, and Merla had received a number of songs in the Spirit for us to sing specifically at this Gathering. The total effect proved to be lovely, harmonious and glorifying to the King of Kings and Lord of Lords. The level of worship from platform to congregation was uniquely beautiful, as we have discovered before in meetings held in Israel. The Watsons are a most gifted couple musically and play something like twenty two different instruments between them, as well as having strong, melodic voices and being very skilled in the area of musical-direction. They lived in Israel for a number of years and faithfully served the Lord in this sphere there and in other countries of the world.

The previous week had seen one hundred and fifty three people meeting on Mount Carmel from a number of different countries, including Uganda, the sole purpose being to wait upon the Lord for His *NOW* prophetic word for the church and the nations. There were several renowned intercessory leaders among the Carmel gathering, including Steve Lightle. This, and the Jerusalem meetings, had been organised by the Rev. Dr. Clifford Hill of Prophetic Word Ministries of England, to whom the Lord had clearly spoken earlier that He would gather the prophets of the nations, first of all on Mount Carmel to receive His Word for today, and then they would take it to a much larger, general meeting of believers from many countries in order

191

to deliver what He had said prophetically on Mount Carmel. Most of the group from East Africa were a part of that larger Jerusalem Gathering.

The evening meetings in Jerusalem majored on worship, very ably led by the Watsons and backed by a team of musicians, singers and dancers. Messages were given by key-speakers, some of whom came from third-world nations. It was quite clear to us that, in many cases, they are far more advanced *spiritually* than the western ones, having undergone persecution, and, in some instances, the total removal of overseas' missionaries. It was fascinating to hear what was going on behind the Bamboo Curtain and in other African countries.

During the daytime there were optional seminars giving biblical teaching on Prophecy; Intercession and Spiritual Warfare; Repentance, Reconciliation and Unity; Israel and the Nations, and Contemporary World Issues. Some of these sessions were led either by teams of speakers or by individual teachers. We bought almost the entire set of cassettes recording the teaching given, and it was of an exceedingly in-depth quality.

I personally attended Lance Lambert's Israel and the Nations seminars and found the background material very helpful for intercession for Israel and the Jewish people. John went to the Intercession and Spiritual Warfare sessions, headed up by Steve Lightle, the late Kjell Sjoberg, Johannes Facius and others of their intercessory partners.

Then, having waited with bated breath all week for the prophetic word given to those who had gathered at Carmel the week before, this was shared on the final Easter Sunday evening, which brought the Jerusalem Gathering to its conclusion. Needless to say, the evil one had sought to bring confusion and delaying tactics to prevent these important messages being delivered to us, and by the time we did receive them fairly late that night, we were somewhat weary to take them in. However, it was good to be able to hear and transcribe them from the tapes after we returned home.

I am including what I consider to be the most important portions of these messages, as follows, in edited form:-

The Rev. Dr. Clifford Hill of the United Kingdom brought the following word from the Lord:

The time is coming when signs of judgment will envelop the nations. Now is the time of preparation … a time of strengthening and harvest. I am among you, the Sovereign Lord of all creation. None can stand against Me. You must declare My Word to the nations. Say, "The things that are coming upon you are the consequences of your own ways. You have departed from My Truth, forsaken My ways, served other gods, bowed down to gods of wood and stone and not acknowledged Me, the Eternal God, Creator of the ends of the universe. Therefore are the nations in disarray; beset by violence, torn asunder by earthquake, fire, famine and disease. These are the signs of judgment. Do not run ahead, wait for My perfect timing, for I will open doors before you and make the way straight, so that you will know that you can do nothing in your own strength, and it will be My name which will be lifted up and glorified before men."

Clifford Hill also brought the following word of prophecy:

"Look to yourselves NOW, you shepherds of the sheep, for yours is the responsibility to carry My Word to the people. Handle My Word with care. Do not despise My utterances, or there will come upon you a famine of words. If you do not humble yourselves and seek My face, I will hide My face from you. If you do not hear My NOW, when you call upon Me, I will

not listen. He that has ears to hear, let him hear what the Spirit says to the churches."

The following was actually the FINAL word which Clifford Hill heard from the Lord at Carmel, although it was delivered next at the Jerusalem Gathering:

"Weep, weep, son of man. Weep and howl, for what is coming upon the nations. You who are called by My name, weep for your nations. Weep before My throne. Call upon Me. Let there be no end to your calling upon Me. For as the tears of My saints wash the broken altar of My Body, healing will come."

Lance Lambert brought the following message:

"I the Lord am shaking all things. I plan to shake the universe itself, skies, sun, moon and stars. I will judge the nations, not only by war and civil war, but anarchy, terrorism and by monetary collapses, and also natural disasters, by earthquakes, shortages, famines, old and new plague-diseases. I will also give them over to their own ways of lawlessness, loveless selfishness, delusion and to believing a lie, to false religion, an apostate church, even to a Christianity without Me. Do not fear; I disclose these things in order that you might be prepared and may stand firm and overcome. For I purpose that you may become the means of encouraging and strengthening many who love Me, but are weak, that many may become strong and find My salvation through you.

Do not fear the power of the Kremlin nor the Islamic revolution, for I plan to break both through Israel. I will bring down their pride and arrogance, and shatter them because they have blasphemed My name.

In the midst of all the turmoil and shaking, and at the heart of everything is My church, joined to Me in One spirit and destined for the throne. You whom I have redeemed and anointed, I will equip and empower and you will rise up and do great things in My name, even in the midst of darkness and evil. For in all My dealings with you, I have always in mind

194

that you should be part of My Bride and reign with Me. This requires a special discipline and training, for I plan that even during all this shaking, the Bride will make herself ready. In the midst of the nations, I have set My Israel, even though they walked in disobedience and transgression in stubbornness and unbelief. Remember, I made them enemies of the gospel for the sake of the Gentiles. I the Lord, I Myself blinded and hardened them that salvation might come to the Gentiles in fullness. Yet, they are still Mine, they are My kith and kin, and I love them. There was no gas chamber, no massacre in which I, the King of Israel, was not present, and now the time has surely come when I shall receive them, for I will reveal Myself to them, and with astonishment they will recognise Me. And to Israel will I turn and melt their hardness and turn their blindness into clear light and tear away the veil from their hearts. Then shall they be redeemed. I have purposed that you shall stand with Me and serve Me in them. Fear not, I love and will protect you and equip you. I the Lord will anoint you with a new anointing and you will work My work and fulfil My counsel. You shall stand before Me, Serve Me with understanding and power and reign with Me during these days. Above all, I call you to be intercessors to serve Me in the hidden place, to receive the burdens which I shall give you and to co-operate with Me until I fulfil My purposes."

David Noakes shared the following word:

"I have called you to enter into the throne-room of the universe, the place where I Who am High and Holy, and Who dwells in eternity, has His seat, from which to give counsel and instruction. To you I say: consecrate yourselves to Me afresh this day and let your hearts resolve to come into My presence and abide there, and not go out from it unless I send you, nor utter in My name anything that you have not heard in My throne-room. No disorder, confusion, darkness or lies can abide there. I have brought you here to cleanse you in the waters of repentance, and to make you holy unto Me

195

and fit to speak My words to My people who are perishing for lack of true vision. Rid yourselves of all double-mindedness. Come out from the worldliness of living that defiles. Learn how blessed it is to be a doorkeeper in My house, and forsake the tents of wickedness. You shall hear My very heartbeat. In the place of consecration and holiness I will share My very thoughts with those whom I have called friends and who love Me enough to want to draw near and be with Me where I am. Commune with My Father as I did and I will make you even as I then was - Jesus in the world."

21. Gates of Brass (Psalm 107:16)

The day after the 1985 Gathering had ended was Easter Monday, and I flew that morning, along with a number of UK participants, to London where I was warmly met at Heathrow by my dear friend, Edna. It was super to see her again, and however long we are absent from one another, such is our friendship and fellowship in the Lord, because we are close prayer-partners, that we take up exactly where we last left off.

She kindly drove me to her home in Derbyshire that same day, and made me very comfortable and warm. I had been amazed just how cold Jerusalem could be in March, but had forgotten that the north of England is even colder and has a much later Spring either than Israel or the South of England! I made her home my main-base for the greater part of my stay, and had an open-return air ticket.

It was lovely to be able to spend a Saturday with my very old friends, Joan and Dudley Nixon, who live only a few miles from Edna, over the border in Yorkshire. I had spent a number of holidays in the Nixons' home during my single years. Dudley and I worked in the same firm in Kent in the fifties and we belonged, together with other mutual friends, to the Workers' Christian Fellowship, which met in my own church once a week in the lunch-hour.

I was able to spend a whole week with our oldest daughter, Anne, in Bristol and attend her church on Sunday. She was most kind in driving me to Bath in the pouring rain and, on another day, still in rain, to Uffculme, the village in which we had lived in Devon from 1979 to 1983. A friend from there

197

invited us to tea, and thoughtfully included one of our elderly Baptist church lady friends in the invitation so that we would fellowship with her at the same time. It was just a little nostalgic returning to Uffculme and driving by our old house, which had not changed outwardly at all. My original curtains were still hanging at the windows, despite the property having changed hands again!

The old struggle of not wanting to return to Africa was raging within. Some of my friends even counselled me to stay in the UK, but I recognised the usual lack of peace when I move out of the will of God, even at thought-level.

From my parents' home on the Kent coast I travelled to London, to stay with a friend with whom I was at Bible college. I felt rather unwelcome right from the start, and spent one of the most miserable weeks of my life in her flat. I had to learn the lesson that, because two people happen to have the same intercessory burdens - in our case, Israel - it does not automatically follow that they will see things in precisely the same light. This friend told me, rather proudly, "I don't like the way you pray!" I felt so crushed that I could not bring myself to respond that I talked to the Lord, not her. She had had two lots of major surgery in the last couple of years and had suffered deep depression as a result. I discovered that she was taking rather large doses of anti-depressants and other prescribed treatment, and that she seemed not to want other people around her in the flat, but preferred to be on her own and go about things in her own way.

The little cash I had in the UK was fast dwindling, so I took a temporary typing job in an office just ten minutes' walk away from my friend's flat. I was suddenly confronted, for the first time in my life, with a battery of electronic typewriters and a word-processor, and had never used either! (The typewriter in Congo had been electric, not electronic.) I managed to master the typewriter, more-or-less, within the first day but was assured by a colleague that, compared to the very latest equipment on the market, my typewriter was very antiquated. I was suddenly overwhelmed by the fact that I was very much the little housewife returning to office-work after many years at home, where a kitchen sink and gas stove were considerably more familiar and easier to handle. I greatly preferred my 'steam typewriter' back in Kenya.

I worked in that office for three days, with every intention of resuming my work after the Bank holiday weekend. However, the relationship in the flat became so silently tense, with the odd outburst from my friend, and tears, that by the Bank Holiday Sunday morning, when I stayed at home to pray because it was very obvious that my friend did not wish to me to accompany her anywhere, that I had to make alternative plans.

Having not received any salary as yet, I had only five pounds in my purse so had not enough cash to travel in order to go and stay with anyone else. There was but one thing I could do, and that was return to Kenya early, via Israel, since I had a valid air ticket worth about £200. I still had long shopping-lists of items unobtainable in Kenya, but the only thing I had managed to buy was a pair of cycle-clips for Paul and some second-hand clothing for myself, much of it winter-weight.

My friend hung her head in her hands over the lunch-table saying that she could not face taking me to Heathrow, so I told her not to give it another thought and that I would get there somehow. I fled to my bedroom sobbing and began packing my

199

suitcase, which I feared would be overweight with unnecessary winter clothes. To my amazement my friend suddenly asked me if I was ready to go, because she wanted to get me and my belongings into the car! Without protest, I quietly got myself and my things together and took them to the car.

Guiltily she tried to apologise, but I reassured her that her actions had forced me into a corner and, although it seemed too early, I now had no choice but to return to Kenya, which I knew to be the Lord's will, irrespective of timing. It was not easy to communicate. I felt badly about leaving my temporary job, and had to scribble a letter at the airport which my friend kindly delivered by hand so that my employers would know as early as possible that I was not able to continue. I also hurriedly wrote one or two other notes to family and friends, but my throat felt constricted and my hand paralysed - I simply did not know how to explain, and wanted to avoid criticism of my friend.

Thankfully I saw that the Bank was open at the airport and cashed a cheque for the balance in my account, which was seven pounds, in order to pay airport-tax on departure from Tel Aviv. The first El Al flight leaving that evening was fully booked, so I had to sit a total of eight hours while I waited around for the second flight, due to take off later that night.

At Heathrow I got talking to Jewish folk waiting for the same flight as myself, and the husband of one family insisted on going to the restaurant to get me food and drink while I guarded his luggage and mine, and would not hear of my paying for anything. Frankly I was beginning to wonder how I could afford to eat, anyway! I was also wondering how to make contact with my long-standing Jewish friend, Joan, who lived on the outskirts of Tel Aviv, after my arrival around dawn the next morning, and whether she would be in a position kindly to put me up for four days while I waited for the weekly-flight on to Nairobi.

The lady at the Information Desk at Tel Aviv Airport was exceedingly pleasant and helpful, and dialled Joan's home number for me free-of-charge. Avraham, her husband, answered and greeted me like a long-lost relative. "Just go outside the airport and you will find our company's car-hire branch-office to your right. Wait there and I'll arrange for a car to pick you up as soon as possible," he said. I could hardly believe the contrast between what I was encountering here in Israel and what I had just left behind in an English Christian home! Joan then came on the line and said, "What a lovely surprise! You are very welcome to come to stay, except that you have come at a busy time and we have all sorts of engagements planned!" I reassured her that I was content just to have a bed and did not expect to be entertained.

Avraham was true to his word. He instructed the branch office receptionist to advance me some shekels to enable me to buy a cup of tea at the airport cafeteria, and then one of his drivers soon came to collect me and take me to his office, where another cup of tea was produced within minutes by a smiling secretary. He then drove me to his parents' home since everyone had left his own house for work or school until evening. I was somewhat wary of going to his elderly parents' home for the day, because I had never met them and just longed to sleep. I need not have been anxious because 'Nanna', as I came to call her (Avraham's dear mother), embraced me so warmly and showed me to a single bedroom that her grandson normally occupied, but he was absent overseas at that time. She told me to rest for just as long as I wished, and to help myself to a bath any time.

201

She thoroughly enjoyed spoiling me, and I was very ready to take full advantage!

Nanna lived with Papa, her married son Issy, his wife June, and their grown-up children. Nanna and I had a long chat that afternoon, and I discovered her to be a wonderful old lady. Papa was as deaf as a door-post and was teased unmercifully by everyone! He did all the household shopping while Nanna kept house and did the family cooking. How the shopkeepers ever managed to get Papa to hear and understand what they were saying was a mystery, but the less he understood, the louder he would shout, I was told, until he had attracted the attention of many passers-by, leaving him quite unperturbed!

One evening the entire extended family was invited out to dinner by another Jewish family from India and, very hospitably, everyone insisted I be included. Our hosts were based in Bombay (now Mumbai) where their company manufactured gas-cookers. The husband and his parents had been life-long friends of Avraham's family and, although they were very rich, with a most palatial-like apartment near Tel Aviv, they were very open, friendly and unpretentious. Again, I was made to feel most welcome.

Joan and Avraham's two lovely daughters, together with Papa in tow, drove me to the airport. Aviva spoke in rapid Hebrew to the young lady-Customs Officer, and got me through in minutes! At the ticket check-in, the lady behind the counter asked me, as usual, why I was forever going in and out of Israel, always travelling by El Al. I simply replied that it was because I loved Israel, the Jewish people, and prayed for them daily, and would not even consider travelling by any other airline. She could not cope with this and, with tears cascading down her

202

cheeks, excused herself with a choking voice and went to get a more senior-male officer to come and deal with me.

The Jews have been such a persecuted people for so many thousands of years that they are always on the defensive, and, indeed, the offensive!

As I flew back to Kenya that night with a 'plane-load of South African Jews, I had that same, all-pervading peace that I had had in 1979 when I returned from my ten months' absence from John. I knew it was right, albeit earlier than either of us had anticipated, and recognised that this was a 'Joseph's pit' experience (Gen. 37:24 and 45:5-8). Interestingly enough, the day before I returned to Kenya, Joan's son had turned on the TV one lunch-hour and, to my amazement, a programme appeared on the screen on the subject of Kenya! A shot was shown of the Nairobi Game-Park, with the Ngong Hills beyond it, very near to our home, and all of a sudden I actually felt homesick, and as though I recognised each giraffe and buck individually!

When the Lord calls one away from one's birthplace and out to another country in which one is to serve Him, it is true that very soon one's birthplace becomes 'overseas' and the land of service, 'home'. I had become very discouraged and disillusioned with the gross sin in some of the Kenyan church but, in trying to turn my back upon it, even temporarily, I was guilty of the sin of throwing back the Lord's call in His face. Time in one's country of origin is very essential, but it must be spent in rest and recreation, sharing with the home-churches for prayer, and preparing to return once more for active service. Since we were not with a mission, as such, furloughs were not regular, and deputation to praying churches was not, therefore,

203

organised. This can be a distinct disadvantage, as one can keep going too long on the field, and discouragement then sets in far more easily. On the other hand, we are free to go and minister or preach where we feel the Lord directs us without reference to other missionaries but, in fact, we worked in close liaison, prayer and fellowship with local African believers, where we could.

As the aircraft began its descent over Nairobi, a Jewish lady asked me if I was visiting Kenya or returning home. "I live there," I said, "but *Israel* is home!" One day these words were to be literally fulfilled.

Just prior to my return, Jay Rawlings, a Canadian who lived in Jerusalem with Meridel his wife, and four boys, visited John and showed his film, 'Gates of Brass' in Nairobi. This film was a docu-drama shot inside the Soviet Union and depicted live-interviews with Russian-Jewish *refuseniks*. The showing of this film brought into being a weekly Prayer Meeting in Nairobi, whose numbers and members fluctuated considerably. This work would ultimately become Prayer for Israel (Kenya).

22. From Beyond The Rivers of Ethiopia, My … Dispersed … (Zeph. 3:10)

In July 1986 we had a visit from Gerald Götzen, who had previously lived and worked in Ethiopia together with his wife. He came to speak to our weekly Nairobi prayer for Israel meeting. He told us about *Operation Moses* which had taken place the previous year, when several thousand Ethiopian Jews had been rescued from the Sudan and airlifted to Israel. He said many more thousands of Ethiopian Jews were waiting to go to Israel, but lack of funding was one of the main causes of delay.

On the evening of 22nd September 1987, a most unusual prayer-meeting took place in one of the Nairobi hotels. The Lord's presence was felt keenly by all and the Holy Spirit was at work in a tangible way. Several of us were given prophetic words and pictures concerning the ministry's future.

The Lord showed us that He was calling us to be involved *mainly by prayer* in the *aliyah* (emigration) of the Ethiopian Jews, with an added sense of our participation in a *secret operation*, and that we were also to prepare the way for *some* to travel to Israel *via* Kenya. We did not understand this, yet I remembered God's call to us in England in 1983 to return to Kenya in order to be involved in Exodus II.

We knew only what Gerald had shared on the subject of Ethiopian Jews, so I set about purchasing a map of Ethiopia and doing some research which re-confirmed there were thousands of Ethiopian Jews living in Gondar in the north-west of Ethiopia, just as Gerald had told us, with yet others scattered to the capital, Addis Ababa, and elsewhere within the country. [1]

Over a period of several years, we got to know various Vice Consuls and staff at the Israeli Embassy in Nairobi and worked closely with them regarding Ethiopian Jews. We enquired how we could help practically, and it was suggested we purchase *winter-weight* clothing for the Ethiopians to wear during winter-months in Israel. I set about buying both new and good second-hand items and these were forwarded to Israel by the Embassy.

By the early '90s we had begun prayer and Bible conferences, weekend retreats and eldership meetings in order to call together those from Western and other provinces of Kenya who had caught the vision to stand with, and pray for, Israel, the Jewish people in the Diaspora and, above all, Ethiopian Jews. In addition, we held monthly 'Highway Prayer-Meetings' in Nairobi to zero-in on the Ethiopian *aliyah* and 'bring them home' in

---

[1] **Ethiopian Jewry:** *No one knows for certain how Ethiopian Jews came into being. Traditionally the visit of the Queen of Sheba to King Solomon (I Kings 10, II Chronicles 9) and their possible union, producing a son, is held to be responsible for the beginnings of both a Jewish people and the practice of Mosaic-Judaism in Ethiopia. The prophet Zephaniah (3:10) speaks of God's worshippers beyond the rivers of Ethiopia as His dispersed ones, and as this prophetic book was written between 636 and 623 BC, this pre-dates the Babylonian exile in 605 from Jerusalem.*

Ethiopian Jews (known as 'Falasha', meaning 'stranger', or 'Beta Israel', the House of Israel) live mainly in Gondar in the north west, with some in the capital, Addis Ababa. Those in rural villages often engage in subsistence-farming, while others are employed in iron-work, weaving, tanning, pottery and stonemasonry. As the title 'Falasha' suggests, they are despised by Gentile-Ethiopians, and they live in separate villages. They observe the Sabbath on Saturdays, and the women keep their hair short and unplaited. Beta Israel are a gentle, dignified people who are very affectionate, especially toward extended family-members. Their young men make excellent soldiers and usually thrive while serving in the Israeli Defence Force but all, young and old among them, long for the day when they will emigrate to Israel to be reunited with their loved ones who have already made 'aliyah' (gone up to Jerusalem). This aliyah is still continuing once a month by air, although numbers have dwindled.

206

prophetic prayer.

We appointed an Eldership Team, but it fell to me to arrange such gatherings, collect fees, set up a book-and-tape stall, and oversee catering, etc. I found these very rewarding, but demanding, and conferences always included a full day of prayer and fasting.

Trinity Fellowship (the mission in which our daughter, Julia, had been working for some years as a teacher) very kindly lent us the use of their wooden-bungalow in Maseno for one retreat. The long journey was quite tiring so, after preparing, eating and clearing away John's and my evening-meal, I began to get ready for bed. No sooner had I undressed than unexpected visitors arrived. A lovely local Kenyan Christian couple came asking for prayer-counselling. The wife was from one Western Kenyan tribe and her husband from another - usually a tricky scenario!

The wife had been ill for some time and was coming under particular spiritual attack in her workplace. As the evening wore on and their story unfolded, we saw this lady was being subjected to strong curses from the husband's extended family and her work colleagues, which is all too common in Africa. She and her husband had an immediate witness of the Holy Spirit that this was the case and cited a number of examples. The Lord graciously ministered deliverance to them as they renounced the power of others' spoken curses and witchcraft (Proverbs 18:20-21), forgave and blessed each by name, even to their receiving Jesus' full salvation (Matthew 5:44-45; Galatians 3:13). They also made sure they repented of any adverse reactions and sentiments on their own behalf. We heard a little later that this dear sister had been miraculously healed of her long-term illness and that she and her husband were rejoicing in the Lord's victory. Hallelujah and *all* praise to His name!

We flew for the second time to the Ethiopian-Kenyan border to pray, this time with our prayer-ministry elders, staying in a school near the border for several days of prayer and fasting, with prophetic-enactment based on a number of scriptures, at the crossing-points and on 'The Highway' from Ethiopia through Kenya. We sought thus to prepare the way for the *aliyah* to Israel itself. To this end the same eldership-team, together with some visiting international intercessors, flew to Addis Ababa, the capital of Ethiopia, for Passover, 1991.

On the Jewish Shabbat (Saturday Sabbath), we were invited to the Israeli Embassy compound in Addis Ababa. By the drive-gates were boxes of walking-sticks deposited by elderly Ethiopian Jews for security-reasons. We laid hands on these and prayed they would soon be supporting their owners as they walked in 'The Promised Land'. Inside the compound were two *tukuls*, which had been joined together to make an Ethiopian-synagogue. A *tukul* is a round, thatched, mud-and-wattle hut.

This was Passover and the Shabbat service was just ending, so we hugged and chatted to a group of women and children nearby. We shared with them, with translation into Amharic, that we had come to warn them to get ready as they would soon be flying to Israel! But what *were* we saying? There were many obstacles to them leaving, yet that was the *'now'* message God had laid on our hearts. Suddenly, an Ethiopian elder came and asked us, "Please could you address *everyone*. They *all* want to hear!"

We had a captive audience of hundreds as men, women and children sat on the terraced hillside and one could have heard a pin drop. Not one baby cried! We read to them from the Prophet Isaiah, chapter eleven and verses eleven and twelve, which our translator read from the Amharic Old Testament, and repeated God's message to get ready to make *aliyah* because He was going to make provision for them to move *quickly*. Many raised their hands and shouted, "Hallelujah!"

Although we were using the Old Testament scriptures, the Israeli security-guards were hovering and becoming uneasy. They indicated it was time for us to leave. We hugged the Ethiopian women on the front row and told them we would meet them in Israel. They looked encouraged and we were all full of praise to the Lord for the open door He had provided.

The next day, Sunday, very early in the morning, a local Ethiopian Christian drove us to a mountain overlooking the city. We had a wonderful and powerful time of intercession and engaged in spiritual-warfare to begin to dethrone strong principalities and powers blocking the exodus of the Jews. The Lord had revealed to us parallels with Zechariah 1:18-21 of four 'horns' and four 'carpenters' and led us by His Holy Spirit to come against specific equivalent political and religious systems obstructing the Ethiopian Jews from departing. Much prayer-preparation lay behind this action long before we set foot in Ethiopia, and the Lord had imparted ministry strategy to us well in advance, with confirmations both from His Word and other believers we met on the ground. Several hours were spent thus on this freezing mountain-top and, as the sun rose, we worshipped, thanked and praised the Lord for His presence, guidance, revelations and honouring of this unique and special time with Him in His service.

Next, we celebrated His Resurrection as this Sunday marked His rising from the dead and sitting at His Father's right-hand (Romans 8:34). We shared Holy Communion and enjoyed a Passover picnic-breakfast before returning jubilant to our guest-house.

On subsequent days we met American Jewish Agency aid-workers and witnessed some of the attractive crafts the Ethiopian Jews were making, including items made from silk. We also moved around the city praying and found that security was very tight, especially at the Post Office. The whole atmosphere was tempered by communism. By contrast, we attended a lovely non-Jewish Pentecostal Church mid-week evening meeting, which was warm, welcoming and lively. We also went back to the Israeli Embassy in Addis Ababa for a most gracious audience with the Ambassador who told us how his country was improving agricultural methods in Ethiopia with great success.

We returned to Kenya after the week was up. We were astounded to learn that at Pentecost 1991 (Shvuot), fifty days after we had prayed in Addis Ababa, *'Operation Solomon'* took place!

This had been a *secret rescue-operation* by Israel about which we knew nothing with our *heads* but about which the Lord had warned us back in 1987. In our hearts we had had a sense of urgency in going to Addis Ababa for prayer-warfare. One matter we had decreed in Jesus' name on that mountain-peak was the toppling of communism and its symbolic statue of Lenin in Addis Ababa. This is precisely what happened as President Mengistu was ousted and Lenin's stone figure keeled over as ecstatic demonstrators went on the rampage!

The Israeli Vice-Consul in Nairobi apologised that he could not tell us in advance about *'Shlomo'* (Operation Solomon), yet when we had seen him back in February one Friday evening (*Erev Shabbat*) at the Nairobi Synagogue he had told me I should go to Addis *quickly!* I replied that we intended to go there to pray in the not-too-distant future, but he insisted we should go *very soon*, and offered me a return air ticket for Passover week. It was as if our job was to pray, while Israel did the rest. What a huge privilege and responsibility! So *now* we understood why the Lord had told us on 22nd September 1987 we were to be involved, mainly by prayer, in a *secret-operation* to rescue Ethiopian Jews and fly them to Israel, the land of their forefathers. We had been preparing with the Lord in Prayer for three years and eight months!

Operation Solomon took place on Erev Shvuot (Friday, Pentecost Eve), taking some thirty hours and involving many shuttle-aircraft. As one landed, another would take off, both in Addis Ababa and Tel Aviv. Over 14,000 Ethiopian Jews were airlifted and, in some cases, all seats were removed so that around 1,000 passengers, minus luggage, could travel in one jet. Babies were born on board, with medical-personnel fully prepared. Not surprisingly, a number of newborn baby boys were named Ivrit (Hebrew). This huge secret operation was planned systematically by The Jewish Agency, The Israeli Defence Force and The Israeli Government, but we give all the glory to the Lord Himself. Some of the new immigrants had not seen their relatives, who had come to Israel earlier, for three to six years.

Hotels were turned into Absorption Centres and Hebrew language-classes were staged for new immigrants, young and old. Buses met the 'planes in Tel Aviv and transported them surreptitiously all night long and brought the new arrivals to their Absorption Centres. Blinds were pulled down over the bus windows during the hours of darkness to ensure the operation was kept quiet and, because special dispensation was accorded to carry this out on the Sabbath, the roads were free of traffic. The video of this operation by *Jerusalem On Line* is most moving and tear-jerking. Even the aircrew, Ethiopian veteran-helpers and soldiers who were involved found themselves weeping unashamedly as these gentle, dignified Ethiopian Jews walked on Israeli soil for the first time.

In January 1992 I changed my first two names by Deed Poll to those the Lord had given me: Batya (meaning 'Daughter of God'), and Sappir (meaning sapphire), thus retaining my original initials of B. S. Within the prayer-ministry we all used Hebrew names to identify yet further with the Jewish people. My birth-names had occultic connotations and I felt uncomfortable with them. I have reason to believe, as does a cousin, that my paternal grandmother may have had a Jewish background, but nominal conversion to Catholicism means no synagogue attendance records exist. However, Romans 11:17-21 reminds us that Gentile believers have been grafted into Israel's olive tree by faith in Yeshua HaMashiach - Jesus the Messiah.

In June 1992 we led a ministry-team of elders to Israel to meet and 'welcome' Ethiopian Jewish immigrants. We visited absorption centres and sat in on Hebrew classes in Jerusalem and elsewhere. We stayed in youth-hostels and used buses to get around as cheaply as possible, taking a strong, folding bag-trolley to carry most of our heavier luggage. Imagine our surprise on visiting a hotel in Safed in the north, which had become an

Ethiopian absorption centre, to be greeted enthusiastically by one man who told us, "Yes, I remember you! You came to the Israeli Embassy compound in Addis and told us to get ready, and here we are! Hallelujah!" There were more hugs and praises to the Lord all round.

We all loved Safed, although recognised that, as one of the four holy cities, peopled largely by Orthodox Jews who embrace Kabbalistic mysticism, that it is spiritually-bound. We prayed at the Citadel and other strategic and symbolic sites and enjoyed being among 'our people', the Ethiopian Jews, as a large contingent had settled in Safed, and the Lord had given us a very deep and special love and compassion for them.

23. I...Will Bring You Again into This Land (Genesis 28:15)

On returning to Kenya after our trip to Israel, I found myself feeling increasingly restless and homesick for Israel. John and I were beginning to sense the Lord was easing us out of Kenya once and for all, and showing us it was His time to prepare to hand over the prayer-ministry to ethnic Kenyans. We saw missionary-leadership was being phased out in many cases.

By now there was a new Vice-Consul at the Israeli Embassy in Nairobi and he surprised us by offering to help us gain residential-status in Israel as 'righteous gentiles'. Occasionally Israel rewards gentiles in this or other ways to mark their recognition of support for the Jewish people.

In the Nairobi prayer-group was an outstanding, mature and gifted man called Reginald Oduor, who had indisputable leadership qualities. He is a university lecturer as well as a talented musician, and was all the more special because he had been blind from childhood. I began a handover early in 1993 and Reginald grasped office practice with alacrity, as he did with everything. Another brother from our Shalom Ministries (Kenya) work agreed to act as Secretary Administrator and be Reginald's reader, etc.

Incredible though it will seem, John and I had returned to the *same* plot on which we had lived in the mid-eighties, although to a newly-built bungalow in the grounds of our old garden. The 'dog-family' were no longer there and our old home was occupied by European teaching staff of a local school. I had no peace about returning to this plot, but there was a chronic shortage of suitable housing at this time. I was especially ill-at-ease spiritually about the landlord (who was a pillar of the local

214

Anglican church) after his previous behaviour toward us. When we went to view the house on the spur of the moment, at the suggestion of the then-tenant, the landlord and his wife had just returned from a splendid lunch with a very senior church minister and he was on a 'high'. He spoke of repentance and putting the past behind us, warmly hugged us and everything in the garden *appeared* rosy. John agreed, therefore, to rent the house, although I was less than enthusiastic, especially as the landlord was acting as if intoxicated, with constant name-dropping of his lunch-host, whom we knew. Events occurred in this epoch, the ramifications of which would have far-reaching effects further down the line.

One morning John and I went to Nairobi for our monthly shopping expedition. He went to the down-town area, on foot, while I concentrated on the more central shops. When we met up for lunch I noticed he no longer had his briefcase, was withdrawn, hoarse and had difficulty speaking. I asked what was wrong and slowly he attempted to describe a mugging to which he had been subjected. Apparently four men approached him from behind, one seizing him by the throat while another relieved him of his briefcase, with the others keeping watch. It was, of course, unwise to be carrying a briefcase, particularly in down-town Nairobi, even in broad daylight.

The briefcase had contained his A.V. Bible with years of underlining and marginal-notes which, in a sense, had far greater value than the cash the muggers had hoped, in vain, to secure. However, local and UK cheque-books, a credit-card and other documentation had been stolen, and had to be stopped with the relevant banks.

In October, my friend Edna visited us in Kenya, bringing John a replacement King James Bible. I have since learnt that she observed strange mood-swings in John. Living with someone daily one is less likely to discern such developments, but I was aware of erratic driving and increasing indecisiveness.

Then, prior to leaving Kenya early in 1993, I began sorting through our possessions in preparation for our immigration to Safed in Northern Israel. We filled our car in order to take items to a Nairobi auctioneer, but were seen doing so by an employee of our landlord. The landlord tailed us in his car and, while we were parked briefly at the local Post Office and John was collecting mail, the landlord put his head through the car-window to speak to me and repeatedly demanded to know if we were leaving on holiday or absconding. I replied, "Neither," but refused to answer further questions.

We were required to give only one month's notice and there were still many weeks ahead before leaving the country. However, he hounded and cursed us, with the all too-willing support of his staff whom he appointed as watchmen of our every activity, and I observed them at the dividing-fence between the landlord's garden and ours, straining to eavesdrop on conversations when friends visited us.

I had severe vomiting one morning after this but, more strangely, deep scratches in the form of a horizontal cross on my inside left calf. John recognised this at once as witchcraft since both these manifestations occurred after our landlord had visited us, extracted from us details as to when we were leaving and why, and I had challenged his spiritual condition, with due warning.

216

We left Kenya somewhat battle-weary late March 1993, having handed over the prayer ministry to Reginald, after a final Intercessory Retreat and having sold off our smaller effects cheaply at a sale for our intercessors.

We flew to the UK for leave via France in the hope of purchasing a second-hand, left-hand drive camper, which we planned to take to Israel. However, these proved too expensive, so we arrived a week later in England, minus a vehicle, and spent some time with my brother in Kent, before buying a right-hand drive camper which turned out to be mechanically unsound. We were based in the camper in the Bristol area, near some of our adult children, for the remainder of our leave and it was sold by a friend after our departure.

We flew to Israel in early July 1993 and stayed first at the Safed Youth Hostel, and then temporarily in someone's empty flat until a first-floor, new-build apartment became available some weeks later. Our landlord was a young, married, observant *sabra* (native-born Israeli) with two small children. Our one-bedroom flat, overlooking the Lake of Galilee at Tiberias, was partly furnished by the landlord, who lived on the ground-floor, and we had to purchase bedroom, office and dining room furniture. Interestingly, our bed-bases came from one of the Safed hotels which had been used previously as an Ethiopian Absorption Centre, the immigrants then being housed in apartments in Southern Safed.

Even in Safed, at 3,000 feet above sea-level, I found the intense summer heat very oppressive, with dripping washing put out on lines on the verandah drying in a short space of time.

Our unaccompanied baggage arrived in due course, and we had to go to Customs in Tel Aviv to clear it. I was rather

217

surprised that all second-hand gas and electrical appliances were dutiable, which rendered our purchases, plus freight and import tax, more expensive than new Israeli ones! The most useful items proved to be a small spin-drier and a caravan fridge.

Once we had settled, we began to think about studying Hebrew. John tried *Ulpan* (direct Hebrew course) once or twice but now in his late sixties, and joining the course mid-way, he could not cope with the pace of the class or the homework. He experienced difficulties in concentrating and memorising. There was a lovely English-speaking Russian immigrant-couple there, however, and we all became close friends.

I fitted in Hebrew between domestic chores using a self-teach book, dictionary and, ultimately, the Old Testament. The enemy of souls detested this, of course, and I would begin to feel nauseous and tired every time, until I took spiritual authority over these attacks and gained the Lord's victory. I also had some coaching in reading and conversation from a South African immigrant.

In 1994 we began attending a unique American Reformed Synagogue in Safed. The rabbi and his wife became real friends who were open and sympathetic toward our Christian stance. The rabbi's wife offered to take over my Hebrew lessons as my tutor was visiting South Africa for several weeks. Her emphasis was more on the conversational and providing new vocabulary but, despite studying three Bantu languages in Africa and my knowledge of French, I found it difficult in my late fifties to string Hebrew words together to make sentences. I was, however, beginning to master reading and writing, albeit slowly.

The synagogue comprised a huge conservatory across the full width of the front of the rabbi's house. Inside it had *a living vine* planted at its centre which thrived in the hot-house conditions.

Sometimes we walked several miles to synagogue on *Erev Shabbat* (Friday, Sabbath Eve), there being no transport after sunset. On other occasions we walked on *Shabbat* morning (Saturday). An inter-linear *Tanach* (Old Testament) and a *Siddur* (prayer-book) in Hebrew/English were collected by each worshipper from near the door and Rabbi would teach systematically for 45 minutes from the weekly *Torah-portion* (the Pentateuch - the first five books of Moses. Torah has been wrongly translated as 'the law' in English Bibles and is a verbal-noun meaning 'teaching'.) Rabbi was an excellent teacher and synagogue became our main spiritual-home in Israel, which I loved even more than the Nairobi Hebrew Congregation Synagogue.

We did hire a car occasionally, which enabled us to attend a Messianic Assembly on *Shabbat* or a mid-week evening Bible-study some distance away. I have very happy memories of all such meetings is Northern Israel.

We returned to the UK for leave in the summer of 1994 and were based in a Plymouth flat. It was good to attend a UK church, although my heart was in the worship 'back home' is Israel. We loved the Hebrew expression in song and Davidic dance-worship.

Not for the first time I was concerned about John's driving in England, and his attention span was becoming shorter as he seemed often to be 'switched off'. Also he would forget to

219

pick up purchases from shops, which had been the order of the day in Israel also.

Early autumn 1994 saw us flying back to Israel, but I felt increasingly uneasy about John's mental and emotional well-being. He seemed peaceful enough in Israel, but there was a strange unreality as if only part of him was fully conscious.

In the October our friends Edna from the UK and Christine (a British ex-Shalom Ministries' elder) from Kenya visited us in Israel. We spent time in Jerusalem and Safed and prayed at, and about, a number of places and situations, each taking our turn at bringing scriptures to focus on. The plan had been for Kenyan intercessors to accompany Chris, but they could not secure visas in time, which was very disappointing indeed.

We rented a car to transport our friends around the North, but felt rather unsure about John's driving much of the time. Israeli roads are renowned for accidents and bad driving, and we had to pray and trust the Lord for daily spiritual and physical protection. It was a challenging time.

By early 1995, when John would be 70 the following November, I noticed he was ultra-forgetful, sometimes confused and remote. On one occasion when driving he failed to notice stopped vehicles at traffic-lights on a very busy, main highway and had a glazed facial expression, as if in a trance. I thought he was probably tired or was slowing down due to his age. I managed to arrest his attention and he regained full-consciousness in time to join the queuing cars, but I pondered on all this with prayerful burden.

I discerned it was the Lord's time for us to leave Israel after almost two years of low-key intercession. We had been visiting an Ethiopian immigrant family in Southern Safed whose two sons had made aliyah via the Kenya 'Highway', with a group of about twenty other young men. They were sorry we were leaving, as were others.

John did not share my guidance to leave Israel and threatened to sit it out alone. He was totally undomesticated and had not so much as boiled a kettle of water for years. He arranged to go and see a local Messianic pastor, but by the time the appointment was due, he had seen we *had* to return to England, which was a relief and an answer to prayer. I did not share my concerns with him about his mental health at that time, as I presumed it was temporary and due to spiritual counter-attacks in Israel and, more specifically, Safed itself.

24. Come ... into The Ark (Gen. 7:1)

In May 1995 we returned to John's native East Devon, near to Sidmouth where he was brought up, in order to purchase a retirement home. A friend kindly allowed us the use of her metal mobile-home in her paddock at Musbury while we were house hunting.

One day while parking our car in Axminster for shopping, I noticed a sign saying, 'Ideal Homes For Sale'. I asked John whether we should take a look, having just turned down another house elsewhere in East Devon about which we had doubts. He was dithery and singularly unenthusiastic, but eventually agreed we could look.

We ended up viewing several new houses in a cul-de-sac, and he decided, to my surprise, that a mid-terrace, two-bedroom one would be suitable. We made an offer which was accepted and we moved in a month later. John had seemed even more tired and confused since we had arrived in England and had told me he could not cope with the purchase of a house and contents, and told me I must handle it all solo, together with all future administration and accounts. He had always checked bank statements and dealt with main financial-matters, so I had no recent experience of attending to these, but had to learn at the double.

We purchased new beds, but found other good quality, second-hand furniture advertised in the local rag, and within a few weeks we were shipshape. We joined a church and met regularly with intercessors there who prayed for Israel and church needs. It was not long, however, before John was not

222

coping with meetings and was nodding off during morning-services. A new pastor also came along whose doctrinal beliefs, in some cases, bothered us, so we felt we could not continue from any viewpoint.

In 1997 I talked to my G.P. about John's health-manifestations and she referred me to the Community Psychiatric Nurse, who thought John was probably suffering from dementia of an Alzheimer's type, although the picture was thought to be mixed. John had always experienced very poor blood circulation, and his G.P. thought it likely that blood was not reaching the brain, indicating a possible addition of Vascular Dementia, which was progressive and deteriorating.

Around this time, John was also diagnosed with Sleep Apnoea and was stopping breathing at night every thirty seconds. Naturally, I was on the *qui vive* and slept very badly. He slept better with the aid of a nasal CPAP (Continuous Positive Airways Pressure) mask, but its noise was as bad as John's snoring, and I found it difficult to get to sleep and remain thus.

These diagnoses meant he had to stop driving and, with an elderly vehicle and insufficient funds to replace it, I felt unable to take over driving. In any case, I could not care for any arising needs while at the wheel. I had also lost confidence, having driven very little in recent years and being unaccustomed to modern UK-traffic and Highway Code. We gave away the car to a local Christian friend and took to walking and using public-transport. So it was that I became a recognised Carer, which became an increasingly full-time and isolating role.

Our second daughter, Sue, married her Andy on 15th August 1998, and mercifully John was able to give her away at Sue's local Anglican Church in Kent. They had a lovely reception in the large garden of the house they had bought and it was a memorable occasion.

The following year, on 15th May 1999, our oldest daughter, Anne, married her Rob in Bristol and John was able, once again, to give her away, although we left the reception early as John tired quickly.

Unfortunately, a *yobbo* had moved next door to us on one side shortly after we had settled, with girlfriend in tow, who then produced two sons in as many years. On the other side a young woman moved in with yet another *yobbo* for a boyfriend-visitor. Loud slamming-of-doors, shouting and amplified drum-beat music, drunkenness and late-night parties assailed us from both party-walls. We endured this anti-social behaviour for over five years, so were forced into a position of reluctantly putting our house on the market in 2000. We loved the house itself and its position in the beautiful Axe Valley, just minutes from the Axe River, where John loved to go and feed the swans and cygnets. He was still fully mobile, but began falling asleep on buses. I would wake him gently a few minutes before we needed to alight, but he would become confused, disorientated and then hallucinate, searching for some imaginary object, such as a penknife, on the bus-floor.

The first couple to view our house agreed to its purchase and planned to move by early October 2000.

An advert in the local paper caught my eye. A local residential care-home, with separate, sheltered, terraced, one-bedroom bungalows in the grounds, had a vacancy. Although this meant down-sizing yet further, I felt it would be suitable for John should he require residential-care later on, and that living there would obviate a major move and enable me to visit him

224

without travelling. He accompanied me to view it and agreed to our taking it from September that year.

What a disaster that turned out to be! A warden was on duty one hour only, six days a week, but the lady-Manager was exceedingly impatient and rude. When the Warden resigned, the Manager accused *us* of being responsible, yet we had rarely seen her, and had a cordial relationship with her when we did. After the Warden left, I saw her one day in the supermarket, so I apologised if we had caused her to resign. She laughed and reassured me, telling me she had taken a much better post elsewhere, and that we were in no way responsible.

John had nowhere to keep a tool-bag, etc., so we asked permission to 'fill in' the open-porch at the front of the bungalow, which was granted verbally by the Manager on behalf of the landlady. A local carpenter came and began to erect a very attractive mini-conservatory with timber-frame and uPVC windows. He had almost completed, when we received a letter in the evening stating the Proprietor did not approve of the structure and that it was to be removed immediately! This Proprietor never once bothered to visit us or introduce herself and, because the Manager was disagreeable and difficult, she fed stories to the Proprietor so that they colluded to work against us. No allowances or compassion had been offered for John's mental illness, and he had unintentionally irritated the Manager's husband one day, which had a knock-on effect. I went over to the Home on one occasion, was kept waiting in the rain while the Manager audibly shouted, "Oh no!" and walked away!

After this it was impossible to settle. We were expected to seek permission even to hang up pictures and were discouraged from wall-mounting cupboards. It was impossible to unpack and we began receiving nasty, unwarranted letters from the Proprietor's solicitors. In our small open-plan sitting-room-cum-kitchen we had our tool-shed contents and one could not move. I was very stressed, became weak and nauseous and lost weight. Even John was awake one night at 2 am. wailing, "What are we going to do? Where can we go?" We had certainly jumped from the frying-pan into the fire, and neighbours were 'hired' by the Management to spy on us and report our every move, or their interpretation of such as in Kenya.

I began packing what had been temporarily unpacked. I remembered walking through a West Dorset caravan-park earlier and noticing one *wooden* mobile-home, fully double-glazed, which was very attractive. So we prayed that, if such detached housing was the Lord's solution for us, at an affordable price, He would direct us very plainly so that no further errors were made.

John's health was relatively stable at that time, so I felt I could manage to go on caring for him at home for the foreseeable future. The Psychiatric-Consultant had warned me, however, that John would 'plateau', then stabilise, then progress and deteriorate to the next plateau, and so on. She prescribed Exelon in the hope of some mental reprieve, but he could not tolerate this drug after a few weeks' trial, and had to be taken off it after suffering a *'funny turn'* which was the first of a series of TIAs (transient ischaemic attacks) or mini-strokes.

I contacted Christian friends to ask them to pray with us about housing, as we were determined not to make any further costly mistakes. Meanwhile, I looked up 'Residential Mobile Homes' listed in 'Yellow Pages' and saw that most were in East Dorset. Only one residential-park existed in the year 2000 in

East Devon and that was near Exeter, off a busy A-road, which did not appeal to us.

I telephoned three parks in the Greater Bournemouth area and made arrangements to go and view several second-hand, fully-insulated, double-glazed, residential *wooden* mobile homes, with the kind help of an elderly Christian friend who willingly took us in her car.

Nothing was suitable on the first park, while the second was not only promising but the park was owned, at the time, by a Christian family with a Brethren background who had built their own chapel nearby. We looked at, and considered, several units for sale, but one we made an offer on was taken off the market.

We returned later for a weekend, and this time viewed an 18-year-old home, fully refurbished, with a double bedroom, study-bedroom, sitting-room, bathroom, kitchen and small porch. We liked it very much and the study, with fitted desk, shelves and cupboards, was perfect for my office-requirements. The owners were in a hurry to move as the wife's father was very unwell in Kent, and they needed to return there as soon as possible to offer support to her parents.

Although we had a six months' contract with the sheltered-housing landlady in East Devon, we could hardly wait to leave, despite having to pay that rent each month until March 2001, and had to forfeit new wall-to-wall carpeting, etc. We agreed to buy the mobile home for a bargain price by faith that we could raise this cash within ten days, because the sale of our Axminster home had been delayed due to the buyer's hospitalisation.

227

Friends and family were wonderful, offering us interest-free loans to top up what we could raise ourselves, and the total reached the exact purchase-price! Our God is a dependable Provider and Mathematician. Praise Him!

Our son, Paul, came to assist with the move. We had already eliminated all non-essentials and placed them in storage to provide space for last-minute packing of the balance. We employed the same one-man removal operator who had moved us out of our house and into sheltered-housing a couple of months earlier. He was so patient and efficient, and nothing was too much trouble. John travelled with him in the removal-van, but asked me to draw him a sketch of the room layout of the mobile home, and understandably seemed very insecure about yet another move while, at the same time, longing to be away from the sheltered housing. Paul and I followed in his car. A Christian friend from East Dorset very kindly came to vacuum-clean our new abode and helped me make our beds, etc.

This home was very definitely the Lord's provision. If only we had known about mobile homes in 1995 when we returned from Israel, or had moved straight into one in 2000, and avoided years of stress! But lessons were learnt and, while East Devon is an area of outstanding natural beauty, so is much of Dorset. John was actually born in Lyme Regis, West Dorset, but brought up in East Devon.

Away from the *'unsheltered-sheltered-home'* John began to relax, especially once I had unpacked all our boxes. He was even able, with our son's help, to wall-mount bathroom-fittings, etc. I ordered him a new metal shed, as wooden ones were banned on mobile-home parks due to fire-hazard, and he used to potter happily out there, with the aid of a fan-heater on cold days.

228

25. Surely Cruel Oppression Turns Wisdom into Mind-Loss (Ecclesiastes 7:7a, paraphrased)

To our chagrin, our mobile-home park changed hands six months after our arrival. We no longer had Christian landlords manning a Park-Office six days a week, but instead had a very worldly-wise businessman to whom residents were mere house-numbers.

He began cutting down mature trees and shrubs in order to make way for extra mobile-home pitches, thus reducing the former 'park' to an estate with park-homes sited cheek-by-jowl. His one interest was cash-flow. Even so, this was the right home and location for that era, without a shadow of a doubt.

We were delighted when our fourth daughter, Louise, announced her engagement, and later her wedding, to her Australian James. They married in Bristol on 24th March 2001, and John coped with the ceremony, managing to give her away, but we did not attend the reception.

I felt we needed, and could only now afford, home-from-home, local, self-catering holidays, so we purchased a 1980-model Elddis two-berth trailer-caravan, despite not owning a vehicle with which to tow it! When not in use, we were able to store it in a designated field on our Park-site.

In May and September 2001, we arranged for this to be towed to Swanage, Dorset, for a combined total of six weeks' holiday, and John loved it. I furnished it as homelike as possible and we stuck mostly to familiar routines as these are very important for dementia-sufferers. The caravan provided a cosy bolt-hole, and we installed a mini black and white T.V. so that we could watch the evening news.

Apart from a couple of falls while walking The Purbecks, John seemed physically well, although he had lost his way one morning to the nearby shower-block, so I accompanied him thereafter.

The following year, 2002, began a series of seven *funnier* turns than John had experienced earlier. These started with convulsions and his face and mouth becoming blue. Sometimes he vomited and lost consciousness. Other times he developed urinary or respiratory infections with dysphagia (swallowing difficulties). On the first occasion I dialled 999 when a paramedic was despatched post-haste, followed by an ambulance, plus our G.P. John's temperature was ultra-low and I thought he was dying. Oxygen was administered, he recovered and the G.P. said he need not go to hospital.

After this, John asked me to ensure he was never again resuscitated. He said he was ready to go to heaven, acknowledged he had lost true quality of life and that it was pointless artificially prolonging it. This was recorded in a new Living Will and his medical notes amended accordingly.

He attended two different day-care centres with transport and activities provided and he looked forward to them. These breaks afforded me a few hours for respite and shopping as I could not leave him at home on his own. Sometimes I arranged for someone to sit with him if I had an unmissable appointment. Otherwise we were always together.

Bus journeys became nightmarish as I had to hold a protective hand over the metal rail on top of the seat in front of John for up to an hour to prevent him banging his head after falling asleep in a near-foetal position. Confusion and disorientation occurred frequently even in our small home, and he began falling out-of-doors from time to time and I found him very heavy to lift.

I had the idea of adding a conservatory to one end of our house to provide extra welcome space and a garden-room for him, so a lean-to model was erected in the summer of 2002. He loved it! It doubled up as a dining and TV room but, after several months, he lost all interest in activities such as painting.

He was able to go for a holiday-break to our daughter, Sue, in Kent a couple of times but, by the time she had a toddler and another baby on the way, John needed full-time respite-care by staff qualified to cope with dementia. I found respite very difficult and depressing, and felt guilty for handing over his care to others. He tried respite in residential care-homes twice, but both were unsuccessful, and he threatened me with having to answer to the Lord for not caring for him at home!

Then, in August 2003, John agreed to undergo a haemorrhoidectomy, despite the surgeon warning the general anaesthetic may cause further deterioration of his dementia. Little did we know that John's predicted hospital stay of a few days would turn into *nine-and-a-half weeks,* beginning with a surgical-ward and then being referred to an elderly-care one because he had, as we had been warned, deteriorated mentally.

I visited daily for the first few weeks, using the students' bus, arriving at hospital by 08.30. Hospital staffing-levels were at a low ebb, so my help in washing and dressing John was warmly welcomed. I felt very *professional* in plastic apron and rubber gloves, especially when I had to bathe his surgical-wound with a saline solution! Double incontinency also was now the order of the day.

   After several weeks of daily hospital visits, I became emotionally and physically exhausted. Senior ward-staff suggested I cut back on the frequency of my visits, so I then went to see John three or four days a week. He was confused and wandering, even by day, and became very aggressive toward staff when 'hands-on' care was essential, and often he refused their supervision, and removed his catheter on a number of consecutive occasions. Then he developed a swallowing-problem once more and all food had to be puréed. All of this combined to produce feelings of guilt that I was spending less time with him on the ward.

   One September day I arrived on the ward to discover he was to be discharged that afternoon by the Consultant. However, John became aggressive with me because I went to the canteen for a quick lunch, which I had explained fully to him. On returning he was puce with rage, shouting that my behaviour was quite unacceptable and that I had no business gallivanting off without him! Sister witnessed this reaction and my consequent distress, and in a few moments I was dissuaded from taking him home again by her, our Social Worker and Community Psychiatric Nurse, the latter having warned me nine months earlier that I should seriously consider residential-care for John because my own health was in jeopardy. I procrastinated over this decision, feeling I had managed John's 24/7 care reasonably well, although I had had inevitably disturbed nights long-term and had become very weary.

   After eight years of caring for John and living in isolation, and while John was still an in-patient, I now felt I

232

could resume attending church. A sympathetic local pastor had been visiting us monthly to share Communion, so it seemed appropriate to worship at his church some twenty-five minutes' walk away. I was very tearful, especially during times of sung-worship. Even at home I had found I could not cope with listening to any kind of music, secular or sacred, as it would cause me to be melancholic, and sob uncontrollably.

At the beginning of John's hospital-stay, the Consultant disagreed that John was behaving aggressively, despite numerous reports from senior nursing-staff that he became hostile when they tried to help him. I felt bullied by the doctors who insisted John *could* return home and that all I needed to do was to contact the District Nurses and Social Services in order to bring in a care-assistant for thirty minutes in the evening to bathe him! However, John refused to allow *any* stranger to do anything by way of personal-care. He was basically a very private individual who, before he became ill, did not even welcome *me*, as his wife, into the bathroom, let alone someone with whom he was unfamiliar. It was me or no-one else, and anyone or anything else produced an aggressive response. Also I was, on the one hand, most reluctant for him to go into care as I had missed him terribly while he had been in hospital, yet, on the other hand, recognised that one person could not cope twenty-four hours per day indefinitely.

I wrote to the Consultant an explanatory letter and had the temerity to interrupt him on his ward-round, but never got through to him. "Your husband's bed is needed urgently"; end of story!

I was counselled by the Citizens' Advice Bureau to adhere to the intervention of the Social Worker, etc, and leave

233

the medical-staff to liaise directly with Social Services, whose sole responsibility it was to come up with funding and a placement, however long it took, which finally materialised mid-October 2003 - nine-and-a-half weeks after entering hospital. This was an amazing answer to the prayers of my new church house-group.

At first I rushed around like a scalded cat preparing John's clothing, etc, with name-tapes and making an inventory for the Home, which was the Home I had vetted and selected earlier. I did not tell John immediately, fearing his reaction, but the Lord honoured prayer in one day. When I broached the subject with John he responded very quietly and calmly, saying I was not to worry, and that one had to go along with such decisions. I think he had probably interpreted this as respite rather than permanent, residential-care, but at least he acquiesced!

I believe the Lord had led me to see and opt for this particular Home, because it was precisely that - a Home, versus an institution, with loving, patient and attentive professional staff. I had every confidence John would lack for nothing in their care, and I could visit when I wished.

26. Not Forsaking Meeting Together
(Hebrews 10:23)

After John went into care I grappled with typical carer-guilt. It all seemed so soon, but I recognised he now needed team-care round the clock, and without a shadow of a doubt this was the Lord's timely provision.

For several months I kept lapsing into depression and tears flowed at the slightest provocation. This was a *living-bereavement*, yet with agonising visits to him and taking him on increasingly stressful outings, before saying a temporary goodbye, followed by more guilt-trips.

The end of 2003 was one of the worst periods: dark, depressing winter days and the dreaded Christmas looming large. I had stopped celebrating Christmas because I had come to view it as a Christianised pagan feast, as is Easter. The commercialisation, spruce trees, eggs and bunnies left me cold and had nothing to do with the events they were meant to commemorate, to say nothing of expense.

The Lord had quickened to me from His Word that the biblical feasts are *His*, not only for His ancient people, but for all who claim to be His through faith in His Son, Who is The Fulfilment of the feasts of the Lord; compare Exodus 12, Deuteronomy 16 and I Corinthians 5:7. Jesus was our Passover Lamb.

Regarding Christmas as a time of celebrating Jesus' birth, it would have been out of the question for shepherds to have been in the field watching over their flock on a late-December night. Rather they would have avoided the autumn-rains around

235

the time of The Feast of Tabernacles and the snow of winter. John 1:14 tells us, 'And the Word was made flesh and tabernacled among us …' Along with many other believers, I accept that Jesus as God's Living Word was, in fact, born during the autumn Feast of Tabernacles and that He dwelt (or *tabernacled*) among mankind on earth.

Revelation 7:15 speaks of The One sitting on the throne *tabernacling* among those who will be redeemed during the end-times Tribulation. I recommend the small paperback, 'The Gospel In the Feasts of Israel' by Victor Buksbazen, published by Christian Literature Crusade, USA, ISBN 0-87508-043-X, It is not so much *when* we celebrate Jesus' birth as *how*, but far more important is His death and resurrection, without which we cannot experience His salvation.

At my new church I found myself greatly looking forward to Sunday services, Thursday house-group and to going out with widows and single ladies for after-church lunch and fellowship on Sunday afternoons.

Then, wham! I had just been welcomed as a signed-up church-member when, in March 2004, I had my three-yearly mammogram and a small, cancerous tumour on my left breast was discovered. I felt numb, particularly as John was manifesting signs of further deterioration at this time. I also went down with recurrent Bronchitis, which adversely affected my ability to sing. Was I dying *before* John, despite his being ten years my senior? I was only sixty-eight and had hoped to have many years of fruitful service, especially after the wilderness ones of full-time caring.

How could I share this news with John, who neither absorbed nor recalled facts and was incapable of offering

236

support? Only the Lord and His faithful praying-people could undergird this situation, so I was thrust totally on Him and them. The living bereavement became yet more intense, as surgery was scheduled for May 4th, 2004. It felt like a double blow.

On the plus side, before receiving this bombshell, I had spent a few special days with my friend, Edna, who came to visit me and, on her way back north, she dropped me off at my paternal-aunt's flat in the Midlands for a brief get-together. Aunty Syb, as she was called, was almost housebound in her sheltered-housing flat and, after my mother died in 1997, I adopted her as my replacement-mother, since she was a childless widow. She was unusually open spiritually and asked me a lot of questions about the afterlife, and she gladly accepted a modern translation of the Bible.

John and I also linked up with our second daughter, Sue, her two-and-a-half year old son, Jonathan, and four month old daughter, Jessica. By now, our fourth daughter, Louise, had a son, Joshua, born three days before Jonathan, and we saw them from time to time. It was super to be proud grandparents. The grand-children addressed John and me as Grandpa and Granna - my choice of title, half-way between Grandma and Nanna! Sue had been working as a Nursery Nurse previously in London, and Louise as a Housing Officer in Bristol.

Before surgery on 4th May 2004, church-elders laid hands on me and prayed for my healing, anointing me with oil (James 5:14-16), at my request. I believe both in direct, supernatural healing and that administered via the surgeon and medical-staff. In the past, John and I had often had the privilege of ministering thus to others and giving God the glory for His

237

honouring of our prayers. However, on no occasion did I or others sense the Lord would heal John, yet He never makes mistakes and His ways are not ours.

I was allotted a side-ward overlooking the Dorset coast, which was such a help to recovery. Surgery went well and hospital-staff were kind, helpful and efficient. A wide, local incision on my left-breast enabled the surgeon to remove an eleven millimetre malignant-tumour, combined with axillary (armpit) surgery to take away two lymph- glands for analysis. All surrounding tissue and glands were pronounced clear, for which I was very thankful to the Lord. I was prescribed an oestrogen-blocker and six weeks' radiotherapy post-surgery, before which Bronchitis hit again.

These bouts of testing thrust me upon the Lord and I was led to repent of the sin of criticism, and seeking the Lord's and others' forgiveness. Drug-therapy disagreed with me, but I had to endure taking it for several more years.

In October 2004 I was invited to the wedding of my ex-Kenya/Israel friend, Marylyn, in Madeira, where she and her family had inherited the home of their late parents who had emigrated there after leaving Kenya. It was lovely to be present at Marylyn's marriage to Colin, an Irish minister who was posted to Spain to tend the expatriate English-speaking Anglican flock. I self-catered in an aparthotel in Funchal for the week and used the time as a little holiday while getting to know one or two local English-speaking guests who had been present at the wedding reception, and I continue to keep in touch with Marylyn's matron-of-honour, Patricia, whose late father and husband were Jewish.

Surprising difficulties arose at my Dorset church which, sadly, were never resolved due to the other party's unforgiveness, so I left toward the end of 2004. Additionally, there was a general lack of vision for, and understanding of, Israel. I missed the support and fellowship of the house-group most of all, and the Pastor confessed he knew of no one in his congregation of around eighty people who was suitable to visit John, which greatly saddened me.

27.Determined Times and Exact Places (Acts 17:26)

Between my radiotherapy and attending Marylyn's wedding in Madeira in 2004, I had been finding living alone in the mobile-home increasingly stressful and lonely, and my G.P. had recommended I move into sheltered-housing.

One Wednesday morning, while praying, the Lord impressed upon me that I was to begin packing up my possessions, despite no outward sign of alternative housing in the offing. As a sheep I recognised my Shepherd's voice and acquired cartons. By a process of elimination (at which I was, by now, something of an expert), I made a start on sorting and packing my worldly-goods, which I stacked in the conservatory.

The following Saturday I received a letter, by second-class post, from The East Dorset Housing Association (but dated on the previous Wednesday when the Lord had spoken to me), offering me a studio-flat in our village! This letter informed me I had one week in which to accept and move, or the flat would be offered to someone else! I went immediately to view the Scheme and hand-delivered my reply to the Housing Association Office, gratefully accepting the tenancy, and began asking the Lord for strength and His pacing to enable me to be ready in time.

The south-facing top-floor apartment comprised a bed-sit, galley-kitchen, bathroom and walk-in store-room, so downsizing was definitely called for, but because there was no through-draught the inside temperature never dropped below 22°C, and the bedroom alcove did not align with the windows.

Many of us found sleeping difficult and airless, but a ceiling-fan helped a little.

I continued to visit John twice-weekly and, with the help of a local driver, took him out or brought him to my flat for meals, etc. However, once he became doubly-incontinent it was preferable to see him *sur place*, sitting in the Home's attractive garden in summer. Often, on sunny days, John would wear his sun-hat indoors - perhaps a legacy from living in Kenya? He felt the cold intensely and would often need to wear a jumper or jacket in the garden, even on the sunniest summer days. He had always had poor circulation.

He was prone to both respiratory and urinary infections, when he showed little interest in getting out of bed or eating. He spent increasing periods of the day napping in an armchair, particularly in the afternoons, but would perk up noticeably when the tea-urn and the biscuit-tin appeared! When physically well, he ate with relish, often helping himself to others' portions as well as his own!

Originally John was able to read his Bible in a limited fashion, but concentration and absorption became more and more difficult, and his Bible would crash to the floor as he dozed-off. As his condition deteriorated further and further, his words became jumbled and unintelligible. Interestingly, whenever he felt insecure or was not wanting to comply with the wishes of the care-assistants, he would speak in tongues (I Corinthians 12:10), which is a gift of the Holy Spirit that he had received in the sixties. The earlier fluency was no longer present, but there were two recurring words: *"shel Abba"* in Hebrew or Aramaic, meaning 'Belonging to Father' or 'Father's'. I would take this up when visiting him by proclaiming to him in

241

whispered prayer in Hebrew, "Yes, you belong to Father, also to Yeshua (Jesus) as well as to the Holy Spirit." One day he added in Hebrew, *"aval zeh kasheh"* (but it is difficult), so I added this to my proclamatory-prayer, telling the Lord it *was* hard (for both of us) and asking Him to give us His grace in the name of Yeshua. John responded to this as to no other words in English. His automatic response to anything said to him in English was "Yes," but he was devoid of understanding or appropriate reaction.

It was not long before John recognised no one in the family at all. It began, understandably, with those he saw less frequently, because of distance or other commitments, but soon included even me, despite regular visits, and also Anne and Paul from Bristol, whom he saw once-monthly. It is particularly hard not to be known by one's spouse, and never easy for offspring either. Dementia shows no mercy.

28. Going Back...Visiting...and Seeing How They Are Doing (NIV Acts 13:35 paraphrased)

By late 2005 people were pointing out that, because John neither recognised me, nor had any recollection of my visits, he would be unaware if I took some time out. It took a while for this idea to resonate, and going briefly to Madeira the previous year had unconsciously paved the way, but still I battled with guilt and what felt like deception and abandonment of responsibility. The Home and Social Services staff told me repeatedly, with limited success, to 'get a life of my own'. I wasn't used to thinking a great deal about personal matters; John was my No. 1 priority.

Thus it was in December that year that I flew to Israel. An elderly friend in Safed, whom I refer to as my *Yiddisher Mama*, dear Edyth Geiger, Founder of the magnificent English Library in Safed, kindly arranged transport from Ben Gurion Airport to self-catering accommodation at a guest-house called *"Beit Shalom"* (House of Peace). However, when I arrived in the airport arrivals' lounge, my driver was nowhere to be seen. He was supposed to be meeting me, bearing aloft a placard with my name on it. Eventually I telephoned Edyth, who in turn called the driver on his mobile, and discovered he was quite a long way away! Another woman had had the audacity to pose as *me* and commandeered him and his car to run her home! This could only happen in Israel, but it caused much anxiety and delay. Edyth told him very firmly to return to Ben Gurion *'hot-wheeled'* to rescue me, which ultimately he did, with profuse apologies, causing a very late arrival in Safed.

My main reason for going back to our old stamping-ground of Safed was to re-visit Ethiopian Jews housed in Absorption Centres there, and to ascertain how they were faring *post-aliyah* (following immigration). Edyth had made arrangements with Absorption Centre-staff, and the same driver, who had collected me from the airport, was on tap for other necessary travel.

I was invited by one such centre to attend a children's Chanukah party and the kindling of the first candle. The Ethiopian Director of this Absorption Centre spent a lot of time with me patiently answering my many questions in perfect English, as he had lived previously in Canada. Israeli staff popped in and out of his office, to whom he spoke in fluent Hebrew and, when fellow Ethiopian Jews greeted him, he conversed with them in his mother-tongue of Amharic. He was a veritable linguist and a most competent leader.

I was made to feel very welcome and at home among these new immigrants and was impressed by the children's command of Hebrew. Everyone appeared to be adapting and settling well into modern-day Israeli life - never easy coming from a rural African background.

After visiting Israeli friends made during our residential-period, 1993 - 95, I moved on to the central region to stay with my friend, Joan, now widowed and living in an apartment. I arrived on Erev Shabbat (Friday evening) in time for a family-celebration of *kiddush*, from which our Holy Communion is derived, and supper. It was lovely to see Joan's three married children and a total of six offspring between them.

The next day, Shabbat, I visited an Ethiopian Jewish believer-couple in their flat and we enjoyed a wonderful time of

244

fellowship and prayer. They now live in Jerusalem, as the central region proved too hot and humid in summer for the wife's deteriorating health and she copes better at a higher altitude. I empathise completely!

My ten-day séjour passed quickly and I returned to England to discover John's recurrent skin problem, where blood-vessels were bursting beneath the surface of his very thin, papery skin, had progressed to another more serious level. He now had a huge swelling on his thigh, which later became cancerous, with other similar eruptions occurring. This condition was diagnosed as Squamous Cell Carcinoma.

When staff washed and dressed him he would flinch in pain when any pressure was applied to these sites, some of which were itchy. However, a hospital-biopsy was out of the question as John could not cope with being hospitalised, because this caused disorientation, a sense of insecurity and unfamiliarity, which all led to his becoming aggressive and uncooperative.

John's Living Will, drawn up in 2002, refusing medical-intervention to prolong his life once his dementia reached an advanced stage, and stating that he was never to be resuscitated, put paid to any such palliative mediation. This made my position even more untenable as I was appointed to be consulted on his behalf on all medical matters, leaving me feeling helpless, and some medics did not appreciate liaising with me.

29. Those Whose Delight is in The Lord's Torah (Ps. 1:2)

South Africa was a country I had longed to visit while I lived in Central and East Africa, 1960 - 1993, but that was clearly not the Lord's time back then.

No sooner had I returned from my Israel trip in early January 2005 than the Lord seemed to lay on my heart that the next venue was to be Johannesburg and that I was to go for Passover, in the April. Suddenly I was becoming a globe-trotter!

I sent for maps and an accommodation-directory and faxed three self-catering properties in Johannesburg, but only *one* replied by telephone. When I asked how near the apartment was to a Reform Synagogue I hoped to attend I was told, "Oh, we go there!"

After exchanging details, the apartment-owner (a convert to Judaism with a Jewish husband) said they would like me to attend their Passover Seder (celebration meal) in their home and accompany them to their *'shul'* (synagogue)! Only Abba could have planned things so meticulously and this was confirmation that this was not a run-of-the-mill touristy trip, but involved spiritual service. I don't *do* tourism!

That sorted out the direct Jewish element, but how was I to contact Gentile 'lovers of Zion'? I met a young South African Christian lady in Dorset whose mother knew of a ministry in Johannesburg called ... wait for it ... 'Shalom Ministries' - the same name as our prayer-and-Bible-teaching work in Kenya! When I got in touch by phone from the UK with the couple leading this organisation, there was an instant rapport and an invitation to their home to meet their group, after which there

246

was to be a large Seder-gathering staged by a Christian radio station, on my first Shabbat in South Africa.

Not surprisingly, the enemy meddled and my luggage was misloaded in Paris after changing flights on the outward trip on 12th April 2006, so I did not have access to my suitcase until the following day! This meant I had to attend my hosts' Passover Seder in the crumpled safari-suit I had travelled in!

It was precious to re-enact this important biblical event and recall with thanksgiving all the Lord's miracles of redemption from all that Egypt represents.

On Erev Shabbat (Friday evening) my hosts took me to their synagogue for the service, after which I was taken to the office whereupon, to my utter amazement, I was invited to preach a ten-minute sermon the following Sabbath Eve!

Next day I attended the Shalom Ministries' Shabbat meeting followed by the Christian radio-station Seder. All races came. There was Hebrew music, singing and dancing. It was very special.

The next few days included leisure activities with new friends at the Voortrekker Monument and Museum in Pretoria depicting the fascinating history of the very pious Dutch pioneers. I saw parallels with the Jewish people's suffering and especially Zionism.

It was lovely to see white lion at Lion Park and to be allowed to caress the cubs.

The Pilanesburg Game Park featured next. Disappointingly, no elephant was to be seen - simply rhino and plains' animals, plus Rock Hyrax, which my companion had never seen. The Park was crawling with Israeli tourists!

To make up for invisible elephant, I was taken to The Elephant Sanctuary, but the weather was too hot for me to participate in the bush-walk on offer.

Then finally, back to the synagogue on Friday evening with 'sermon' at the ready, bearing the same title as this book. I began by reading a prophetic scripture before giving some background personal information, including my marriage to John and five instant, lovely children, before going on to describe our involvement, mainly by prayer, in 'Operation Solomon' - the *aliyah* of nearly 15,000 Ethiopian Jews airlifted to Israel.

The congregants sat with rapt attention as I recounted the story and told of our living in Kenya and Israel, culminating in my sadness at John's dementia and residential-care. They were clearly moved. Even the Chazan (Cantor) came up to me, hugged and kissed me on the cheek saying kindly, "You are a remarkable woman!"

One young man did likewise, adding, "When I came to Shul tonight something felt different; an unusual peace and special ambiance which *you* brought!"

Another lady said, "I could have listened to you *all* night!" All glory to Messiah Yeshua! This was His Divine Appointment.

On my final Shabbat I was invited to speak to the Shalom Ministries' afternoon gathering, which produced a very warm response and a number of questions. How marvellous it was to be with likeminded folk. I would miss this level of fellowship when I returned home, and would be counting the months before another visit, D.V. I would happily live in South Africa were it possible and God's will.

248

30. Precept upon Precept; Line upon Line, …
(Isaiah 28:10)

One huge encouragement during 2006 had been the discovery of Precept Ministries' inductive Bible study methods and materials. These were exactly what I had been seeking for the past forty-nine years, as most daily Bible-notes proved too brief and lacked the depth and challenge I needed.

John and I both loved and taught God's Word and I learnt a lot from his in-depth teaching. We had made morning Quiet Times a priority for ourselves, our children and others to whom we were privileged to minister.

Precept Ministries UK provide excellent, sound study-materials which are life-changing and, very importantly for me, pro-Israel. Discipline and commitment are essential, but most rewarding, and it can be hard to put studies down. I certainly recommend sending for a resources' brochure from Precept Ministries (see back of book for details.)

There are overseas' branches and a selection of materials is available in different languages. Also study-groups have been formed at home and abroad, with one-day or residential-courses on offer, plus tours to Israel whose emphasis is on Bible-teaching. The International Headquarters are in the U.S.A. where this ministry was founded principally by Kay Arthur; while in the U.K., Nigel Watts is the European Director most ably assisted by his wife Molly and a team of dedicated helpers.

In the autumn of 2006 I spent four nights in Clevedon, North Somerset, with the goal of researching rented-sheltered housing and testing public-transport availability. I felt that once

John had died it would be preferable to live nearer Bristol-based family members, although Louise, James and their two boys were to move to Australia. (Three of our four girls had attended boarding-school in Clevedon and I had convalesced there in 1977 after major surgery in Kenya.)

I met a variety of Christian and secular Clevedonians. The town had developed and changed, of course, but it still appealed as an ultimate residential-venue.

Then I was diagnosed with Diabetes Type II which can be brought on by stress, at least in part, just as some medics think some cancers can be provoked by stress. Doubtless stress has much to answer for.

John was continuing to deteriorate and had an anti-psychotic medication administered covertly, with my reluctant approval, to avoid staff and residents being injured, after one senior care-assistant suffered thus during hands-on care at night.

A year after my Clevedon recce, I followed this up with a further week spent in the guest-room of one of the sheltered-housing schemes to which I had applied for a flat further down the line.

I spent the week attending Christian meetings and services and checking local facilities, etc. Toward the end of the week, the Housing-Scheme Manager, in the block of flats where I was staying, invited me to view two vacant flats, one of which was sea-facing on the second floor and the other garden-facing. I had not anticipated this as I had already turned down several offers because I was not reckoning on moving until *after* John's ultimate death. This week was meant to be further preparation for some point in the future.

Then, an unexpected bombshell and predicament! On returning home I had a phone call from the Scheme-Manager offering me the sea-facing flat! My friends all believed it was the Lord's time for me to move on and pointed out that I could still visit John with one of the Bristol children on a monthly-basis, which was the frequency now counselled by the Home. What to do?

After a sleepless night spent praying, with others supporting me in prayer, it certainly *looked like* the Lord's appointment, yet why *now?* Psalm 31:15 reminded me, "My times are in Your hand."

So it was that on the eleventh of December, 2007, I moved from East Dorset, with all its bittersweet memories of joint-activities and of going places with John, to North Somerset. Despite moving from one studio-flat to another, the Clevedon flat was smaller and a different shape. This meant getting rid of excess furniture of a horizontal design and ordering replacement-items of a vertical design, floor-to-ceiling, as horizontal wall-space was lacking.

While awaiting the arrival of the newly-ordered furniture and the carrying out of refurbishment work on my kitchen, along with all others in the scheme, I spent two weeks self-catering in Madeira seeing my English Messianic friend, Patricia.

In Funchal, where Patricia lives, opportunities arose to share God's Word with English-speaking visitors and local residents at her regular Thursday-morning meeting held in her apartment. We also celebrated the *Kiddush* on Friday evenings in her home, to which local friends were invited.

Originally Funchal had a sizeable Jewish community, so it was sad to see a near-derelict synagogue being left neglected

251

and open to the elements. Patricia would love this building to be restored and used for the Lord's purposes one day, but several miracles would be needed first.

31. Restoring The Locust-Years (Joel 2:25)

During my fortnight's stay in Madeira, the Lord began speaking to me about re-visiting South Africa for Passover 2008, but this time my trip was to include Cape Town.

I had no contacts in Cape Town, but my Shalom Ministries' friends in Johannesburg kindly put me in touch with a lady who worked full-time with Jewish women.

My self-catering apartment overlooked the well-known Table Mountain and its cable-cars. I was invited to share my testimony at six messianic meetings, including a messianic congregation whose premises are laid out in the style of a synagogue. I met some wonderful people in Cape Town among whom were Lorrain Fleurs of The Society for Distributing Hebrew Scriptures and her sister, Judy, who kindly took me to the Kirstenbosch Botanical Gardens one day. We had a most enjoyable time with wonderful unity, fellowship and eating lunch together out of doors.

All too soon my eight days were over in Cape Town and it was time to fly on to Johannesburg, where my dear friend, Channah, met me at the airport. Everyone was busy preparing for *Pesach* (Passover) and I attended three different *seders*, which was a great privilege and blessing.

Once again I was invited to bring a message to two Shalom Ministries' Sabbath meetings. Roy and Sheila Burke, who head up this ministry, ably assisted by their daughter, Dorothy, have very full lives which incorporate Hebrew-teaching by Sheila. Even so they managed, with Channah, to take me to the Roodeport City Museum depicting pioneer-

253

history, which was most interesting. Also to the Krugersdorp Game Reserve and Lion Park. We shared lovely meals and fellowship together.

Channah kindly invited me to stay with her in her Johannesburg retirement-village apartment. Such villages are very popular in South Africa and they offer good security. We are both 'early-to-bed', 'early-to-rise' people and have much in common, not least our love of the Jewish people and the uniquely special Hebrew language.

An invitation to speak was also given to me from a pensioners' CFI (Christian Friends of Israel) group in Pretoria held in the sitting-room of one of the key-members in her retirement-complex flat. It was lovely to witness the strong commitment these elderlies had to Israel and the Jewish people, especially through intercessory prayer. Sharing with them was such a privilege.

Time passes rapidly when one is enjoying likeminded company and activities of mutual interest, despite remaining 'on-call' via my mobile for any emergencies arising from John. Departure-day was looming once more and I needed to get back to the UK and relieve Paul from 'holding the fort' as far as John was concerned. It was never possible, nor desirable, to switch off completely from my caring-rôle and sense of duty wherever I happened to be.

32. Streams in the Arava   (Isaiah 35:6)

By the summer of 2008 John's walking had become slow and laboured and he was spending hours staring into space or dozing. His skin-tumours were large and spreading. He had by then been in residential-care for five years whilst most clients in the Home survived only for a couple of years or less. Watching his progressive decline became more and more difficult and I could understand, in part, why some relatives rarely, if ever, visited their loved-ones suffering from advanced dementia. He was constantly fearful of falling and hung on to people or furniture tightly. Falls occurred fairly frequently.

Our son Paul had, by now, become engaged to a very special Brazilian Christian lady called Vania, who is a keen evangelist and intercessor. I am very fond of her, as is all the family, and she had a deep spiritual-burden for 'Mr John' as she respectfully referred to him, and visited him with Paul and me regularly.

From the nineteenth of December 2008 to the eighth of January 2009 I spent time in Jerusalem, Arad and Safed self-catering with a friend, visiting old and new Israeli friends and, most importantly, engaging in intercessory-prayer.

In Jerusalem, we visited my old Ethiopian friends and enjoyed fellowship and prayer in their East Jerusalem apartment. They have a small Ethiopian congregation who meet in Jerusalem on Friday evenings using rented accommodation and a hired vehicle to collect and return everyone, there being no public transport on Shabbat from dusk-to-dusk.

We also went to the Western Wall in the Old City on Shabbat morning, to which we were able to walk from our rented flat. It is always wonderful to soak up the atmosphere at The Wall with hundreds of Jewish visitors and residents who have gone there to pray and celebrate the Sabbath.

From Arad I went with three friends by hire-car to Eilat on the Red Sea. To our amazement we witnessed tank-line up and mass-troop movements in preparation for Israel's justified retaliation upon Hamas in Gaza, who had bombarded Israel relentlessly for eight years, traumatising citizens. (*Chamas* in Hebrew - chet mem samech - this word means oppression, cruelty, injustice, rapine, corruption, brigandage. When used of the Hamas Movement in Gaza the Hebrew spelling is chet mem aleph samech and is an acronym for Islamic Resistance Movement meaning bravery, enthusiasm.) We were stopped briefly by friendly I.D.F. soldiers at a desert road-block on our return in the dark and had to make a detour back to Arad.

I loved the drive through the Negev Desert (or Arava) and could see how these miles of emptiness could be such an advantage to new immigrants. We visited an agriculturalkibbutz and found the modern mud-houses fascinating. I could not help but envisage thousands of pastoral-Ethiopian immigrants living in such houses on small-holding plots, versus modern apartment-blocks in towns and cities.

These houses are perfect for a desert climate as the mud provides excellent insulation from intense heat. The ones we saw on the kibbutz had windows, doors, electricity and water, although a more permanent and sustained water-source would be needed if thousands were to settle there in the future. Sturdy palm-branches were utilised to make the dome-like structure

256

over which the mud was applied to form the walls and roof, so the materials were local and gratis. The kibbutz grew crops and reared domestic animals very successfully, although naturally the climate required regular irrigation.

The North of Israel came next with a base in Safed (where John and I had our home 1993 - 1995) but we made a prayer-journey to Karmiel, Rosh Pina, Tiberias, Metulla and Kiryat Shmone. A warm welcome was given to visit three absorption-centres in Safed, including individual apartments within the centres where Ethiopian families were housed. Some of the women make beautiful, brightly-coloured baskets while others embroider, and we sat in on an *'ulpan'* (Hebrew language-class) in one of the centres. It was good to be hearing Hebrew again, especially as a young Ethiopian woman was the teacher! Her Ethiopian pupils ranged from around twenty-years old to the grey-headed, the latter struggling with the complexities of Hebrew.

A number of Ethiopians are illiterate which presents a barrier to mastering written Hebrew and therefore holds them back from complete integration, to say nothing of employment. However, those who make *aliyah* as children usually do well and a number have acquired university-degrees. Amharic is, in fact, a Semitic language, and is very complicated.

I had been sensing the next port-of-call, as the other side of the Ethiopian coin, was to re-visit Ethiopia, and in particular to go to Gondar, in the North West, to which I had never been. It would make economic sense to include Kenya, which John and I had left sixteen years earlier, and, due to Kenya being well on the way to South Africa, to combine all three African nations in one trip. Quite an undertaking!

257

So, much to pray about and prepare for, as time in my beloved Israel came to a close, but not before attending a messianic fellowship in Tiberias one Shabbat. English-translation was provided, but I love listening to the Hebrew and trying to recognise vocabulary. In fact, I love everything about true messianic-worship and feel at home *only* in such fellowship-meetings. It is what I miss most in England.

33. The Remnant ... from Cush (Is. 11:10-12)

It was such a delight to attend Paul and Vania's uniquely lovely wedding in Bristol on the fourteenth of March 2009. They had had a civil wedding in Brazil some months earlier, but Vania had to remain there until official paperwork was completed in the UK for her to return to England. They did not regard the civil ceremony as having spiritual validity and did not live together until after their church-blessing.

On the following sixth of April I flew to Addis Ababa where I was met by my Ethiopian Jewish friend from Jerusalem and a mutual friend from Addis Ababa who is a key, senior figure from the Ethiopian Jewish Community. I used to correspond with the latter when we lived in Kenya.

My friends drove me to a Christian guest-house I had used during the Kenya Team's previous visit, where I now spent one night before flying on in a medium-sized plane to Gondar in the North West of Ethiopia. My Jerusalem friend was due to arrive later in order to care for her sick father, but this matter so preoccupied her time that we linked up at my rather sleazy 'hotel' for a mere three and a half hours.

Sadly, my other local Ethiopian Jewish contact never materialised due to pressure of work, but what could have been written off as a wasted week was actually a prophetic-enactment. Just as I spent that time waiting, that is exactly the position of the Beta Israel communities in Gondar and Addis as they wait, with limited hope, to be reunited with their loved-ones in Israel. However, I had plenty of time to pray, especially at night, as tourist-guests were slow settling down to sleep.

259

I did manage to commission a taxi to take me to the Beta Israel Children's Feeding Centre where a Passover service was in train. Two Israeli rabbis led the service in Hebrew, and the room (set up as a synagogue) was packed, with a very large contin-gent of children. The community was not resident at this centre, but lived in their own local homes in the vicinity.

I returned to Addis and flew on to Kenya, where our missionary-teacher daughter, Julia, met me at the airport. It was good to spend three weeks of her school-holidays together, during which time we went on safari to our old stomping-ground of Nakuru and also to Athi River, where we enjoyed watching flamingos and game. While in Nakuru one of the ex-Shalom Ministries' elders, Joseph, and his wife, met us and it was just like old times! Julia and I also visited our old house at Lanet and were shocked to find it abandoned and dilapidated.

Also in Nairobi I visited Reginald and his wife, Lilian, in their home for lunch one day, and on another to attend their prayer for Israel meeting. (Reginald was the brother who took over Shalom Ministries when John and I left in 1993.) The Lord had been so good to us all in the sixteen years of absence. It was splendid to renew fellowship with these dear ones.

Lots of changes were observed in Kenya: so many vehicles, people, houses, markets and activity everywhere. However, anti-malarials upset my digestive-tract and at times I felt unwell in Kenya. When we lived in Kenya I took anti-malarials only when holidaying at the coast. At an altitude of 6,000 feet in Nakuru it was then considered unnecessary to take prophylactics, but now they are recommended at all altitudes.

Julia drove me to Nairobi Airport for my plane to Johannesburg on the sixth of May, where Channah met and drove me to her new retirement-complex apartment in Pretoria. It was wonderful to see her and be in South Africa once more.

Within a few days we were attending excellent seminars by Brad Scott of Wildbranch Ministry and Rico Cortes of Wisdom in Torah Ministries, both based in America. It was tremendous to delve into the Hebrew biblical-text and to partake in their many years of Torah-study. Rico is himself a Jewish believer.

Once again I was invited to give a message entitled 'Bride-Readiness' to the Shalom Ministries' Johannesburg group and another to the C.F.I. pensioners' group in Pretoria on 'Floating Our Ark'.

Channah spoiled me by taking me to the Kruger National Park, but the 'cats' proved shy, just as they had in Kenya. We stayed at a holiday, self-catering establishment overlooking a river, outside the Park, which made for a lovely break.

Sadly, I struggled on and off with gastric problems, which culminated in me being admitted to a five-star hospital in Pretoria where I was attached to a saline drip for three days. I was extremely ill and lost twelve kilos. This delayed my return to the UK by several days, but I had an Assisted Passage, with wheelchairs and buggies at my disposal, which whizzed me from A to B in no time.

A few days after my return home I visited John four times in the next month. The huge tumour on his thigh was ugly and suppurating and he developed others on his elbow and underarm. He was more gaunt and frail, had lost some weight (which seems to occur with many dementia-sufferers, and this may be connected with its effect on metabolism in the advanced

261

stages, perhaps). He was continuing to wander by day through the Home, apparently searching for someone or something. Could it have been his late mother or me, whom he no longer recognised?

Calls from John's Home were fairly frequent to report on his latest crisis. A month after returning from South Africa he had the beginnings of a cataract in his right eye, and his left eye had been red and sore long-term. However, it was difficult for care-staff to administer eye-drops as he did not understand what they were doing, so he refused to co-operate much of the time. He continued to have nasty falls with worrying regularity.

The French have a saying: 'ça change les idées', literally, 'it changes the ideas'. To change mine, and have some diversion, I went on coach-day trips from time-to-time. The downside was that most other passengers comprised couples, families or groups of friends, and somehow this fact is emphasised when one travels alone and is missing one's spouse. The same scenario occurred on bus-journeys when I went farther-afield for shopping-trips.

Our oldest daughter, Anne, had an operation on her thyroid that summer of 2009 due to abnormal cancerous cells being discovered. Family sickness seemed to be the order of the day, but mercifully, in answer to much prayer, she has made a complete recovery and her voice-box has returned to normal. Of course, no family sickness or news could ever be relayed to John in recent years because he no longer knew our names or our relationship to him.

In the autumn, as a further diversion, I joined a weekly church-walking group and another, less frequent, secular one locally, but met several Christians who were members of the latter. Sometimes we wound up at a pub for lunch on the more distant-rambles. These provided both congenial company and good exercise.

The Lord had given me a prayer-burden for Clevedon when I moved there at the end of 2007, and a friend and I met from time-to-time to pray together. While I was in South Africa, a brother with the same concern began Prayer for Clevedon (or P4C) which met in his home once a month and a prayer-breakfast was also staged each month at the Town Hall. I was invited to join P4C together with the friend I had prayed with earlier and we are witnessing much blessing in this work. Speakers are invited to address the breakfasts from time-to-time and/or keep us abreast of needs in the area by e-mail so that we can pray intelligently. I look forward very much to meeting with the very special Pray-and-Planning Team and we pray together in close unity and fellowship.

34. God Sets The Solitary in Families (Psalm 68:6)

On the occasion of my two UK grandchildren's October 2009 half-term, I went to stay, by choice, in a self-catering flat near to their Kent home, so as to spend time catching up with them. I am very fond of Sue, Andy and their two lovely children and, indeed, we are very blessed with our married children's choice of spouses. It was good to accompany Sue and her family to local parks, National Trust properties and the Thanet coast, where my late parents used to live.

No sooner had I returned from Kent than the Home rang me to say John had developed yet another tumour on his back, and that they were endeavouring once more to administer drops to John's extremely red-and-sore left eye. A biopsy was carried out in-situ on the thigh-tumour by a local hospital-dermatologist visiting the Home one evening in early December. Results confirmed, as mentioned earlier, that these were cancerous, as suspected.

Paul and I visited John on Boxing Day, which had been the order of the day when I was in the UK. John was very sleepy, and increasingly this was the case, especially after lunch when relatives were encouraged to call.

Early in January 2010 I developed severe lymphoedema on my left breast which left me very scared, despite annual mammograms giving good results. I attended Frenchay Hospital's breast-care department, in Bristol, and was reassured that the lymphoedema would right itself in time, but it was very tender and uncomfortable in the interim. I was told an earlier-than-usual mammogram was not required, and indeed, after

264

several weeks, the swelling subsided, and the subsequent mammogram was normal. I was very relieved and thanked the Lord.

Then I developed kidney-stone symptoms, saw the Renal-Consultant surgeon who suggested I wait to see if things plateaued or whether surgery became necessary. An operation would be essential in my case because the 7mm stone was lodged in the lower pole on the left-hand side of my horseshoe-kidney, which would mean making a hole in my back above the waist to extract the stone. I had hoped it would be removed by ultra-sound, but that would be out-of-the-question with a horseshoe-kidney as was keyhole-surgery.

On the fourth of February I took delivery of a laptop! A Jewish Messianic friend had spent some time persuading me I needed one, disregarding the fact of my being computer-illiterate! I had seen for some time that to be able to send and receive e-mails from home and abroad would be a great advantage, as sending letters by post was slow, expensive and unreliable. A local friend kindly got me launched. How timely it was because within days I would need to send and receive emails by the dozen!

35. Precious ... is the Death of His Saints (Psalm 115:15-18 NIV)

Two days later, on the sixth of February, John had a heart attack and a new downward-spiral then began. The Assistant Manager of the Home kindly gave me her home telephone number to call any time, despite officially being off-duty over the weekend. She told me I would need to transfer John to an alternative Home which offered nursing care, which I had not anticipated.

Paul and I drove to visit John. He seemed to have aged markedly since our January visit. On the third of March, four days after our visit, John had an extremely bad fall, resulting in a broken arm, followed by a stroke which paralysed his left side, requiring four care-assistants to move him. The Home-Management had no alternative but to send him to hospital, and to refuse to allow him to return.

The nearest hospital to me to which the Dorset Ambulance Service was permitted to transport him free-of-charge was at Salisbury, but still a long way for me to get minus a car.

I spent the next day phoning all the Clevedon residential-homes and only one could offer full-nursing care for a dementia-sufferer. Paul, Vania and I drove to see this Home on the sixth of March but, whilst a provision for residential-care had to be made as a legal requirement, in which Social Services were involved, we all knew John would *never* go there. We all sensed the Lord was definitely taking John Home to Himself, so visiting the new place seemed unreal.

Our next stop was John's old Home on the Dorset-Hampshire border to collect his belongings, as he had been sent to hospital with nightwear and a toilet-bag only. After visiting John at this Home since October 2003 (almost six and a half years), it seemed equally surreal that this was our final time. We thanked the Staff in person, and I wrote and sent two large boxes of chocolates, although that felt inadequate in return for all their sacrificial care.

Finally we drove to Salisbury Hospital and found John quite dehydrated, as he could not manage to help himself to the water-jug on his locker. He looked pathetic sitting in a chair, wearing a hospital-gown, on a chilly day, with no dressing-gown or slippers.

We prayed at length with and for him and knew we would not see him again on this earth. The hospital staff had swabbed him for MRSA (Methicillin-Resistant Staphylococcus Aureus), which proved positive, so he had brought this virus into hospital with him, in spite of rigorous hygiene-standards observed in the Home.

I telephoned the Ward at least twice daily. He was unable to eat or drink, take medication or be active in any way. Once put to bed he remained there, his Living Will ensuring he received no medical intervention, in accordance with his wishes. The duty-doctor informed me on the eleventh of March that they regarded him as a dying man and John passed into His Lord's Presence in the small hours of the twelfth of March, having contracted hospital-acquired Pneumonia.

I found it very hard that, having given the Ward Staff my landline and mobile telephone numbers, they failed to ring me to inform me of John's death and, instead, phoned Paul. When I called the Ward very early on the twelfth, his death was already a *fait accompli* and, although I had been expecting it, nevertheless it came as a shock, rendering any further contact impossible. I could but worship the Lord that John would never suffer again, while weeping initially.

One blessing in being in Salisbury was that John's brain-tissue donation for dementia-research purposes was made very straight-forward as the Chief Anatomical Pathology Technologist, already assigned to undertake this post-mortem procedure, was based at Odstock Hospital in the Salisbury district. The donation was then transported to the South West Brain Bank at Frenchay Hospital in Bristol. The report on their diagnostic investigations, received three months later, revealed John had suffered from Alzheimer's Disease, Lewy Body Disease and Moderate Small Vessel Disease.

The next couple of weeks were extremely busy, informing others of John's death and appointing a funeral-director. Paul took me to our local Crematorium to check on facilities and confirm Memorial-Service arrangements for the twenty-ninth of March at eleven thirty a.m. - delayed to enable Julia from Kenya and Louise from Australia to fly to the UK as it was very important to me and them to have all the family together.

John's Memorial Service would not be a run-of-the-mill one. He would have wanted it to include elements from Kenya (where he spent over forty years, apart from UK leaves) and Israel, his final overseas destination. I felt it essential to have three key features: the blowing of a shofar as a call to celebration of John's life and spiritual service; the recording of the Israeli National Anthem, and Davidic sacred-dance, around the theme

268

of a rainbow of promise that he had gone to heaven. The rainbow was depicted in a length of silky, multi-coloured fabric which the dancer, dressed in white, would hold aloft as she danced.

I had had a coffin-cover made in white crushed velvet with the crest of Sidmouth, Devon, and Kenyan and Israeli flags attached to its top. It wasn't easy locating a shofar-blower, but two emerged at the eleventh hour via The Messianic Testimony, as did a sacred-dancer from Portishead, after much prayer and many phone calls. Reginald recorded three songs in Kiswahili

O love that wilt not let me go,
I rest my weary soul in thee;
I give thee back the life I owe,
That in thine ocean depths its flow may richer, fuller be.

O light that followest all my way,
I yield my flickering torch to thee;
My heart restores its borrowed ray,
That in thy sunshine's blaze its day may brighter, fairer be.

O joy that seekest me through pain,
I cannot close my heart to thee;
I trace the rainbow through the rain,
And feel the promise is not vain, that morn shall tearless be

O cross that liftest up my head,
I dare not ask to fly from thee;
I lay in dust life's glory dead,
And from the ground there blossoms red
Life that shall endless be.

George Matheson (1842-1906)

269

and English, which provided a contribution from Kenya and our earlier Shalom Ministries (Kenya).

Guests commented that the service was very unique and special, and Tim Simpson of P4C led it most sensitively, while key friends from near and far participated from the front, including Gordon Smith from Dorset, who gave the Address. The hymn, O Love That Wilt Not Let Me Go, was a moving part of the service accompanied by dance.

The buffet-lunch reception for around 50 guests was held at a local hotel and was expertly catered for by the chef and his assistants. After lunch my friend, Edna, showed slides of her visits to us in Kenya in more pleasant times, and before tea the 'Operation Solomon' video was shown to testify to our privileged, spiritual-involvement behind the scenes.

I was exhausted by the end, but the Lord had upheld me. My son-in-law, Andy, videoed most of the service and Paul took digital photos at both the service and reception. A Book of Remembrance is in the throes of being compiled to mark happy memories of yesteryear contributed by friends and family.

Had I not been able to go through these years of trial with the Lord I cannot imagine how I would have coped, particularly as these covered a long period of suffering for John. It can be harder for carer-relatives watching the slow decline of their loved ones, because the cared-for become unaware ultimately of its progressive nature.

And so, after thirty-eight and a half years of marriage, fifteen of them as a carer, to widowhood ..... The sound of caring resonates no longer. It is deafeningly silent. It had been one thing to be a virtual widow for six and a half years, but to be an actual one would take some adaptation.

270

Now there was a sense of finality, yet with the hope of going to where John had gone as a committed believer in, and servant of, the Lord, yet I am in no hurry!

36. Plans to Give ... Hope and a Future
(Jeremiah 29:11)

Several activities have pre-occupied my time these past few months. On the eighth of February 2010, several weeks before John's passing, I was invited to lead a Clevedon-based Precept Bible-study group. This invitation was followed shortly after John died in mid-April by another from a couple I had met earlier from Nailsea. Both groups were following the New Inductive Study Series on the book of Revelation entitled, 'Behold Jesus Is Coming' by Kay Arthur, and all were very committed and enthusiastic. Preparation for leading these studies took many hours, but was very fulfilling and the course-work occupied the equivalent of most of two school-terms until the summer holidays. The two groups have now merged in Clevedon, meet fortnightly, and we are currently studying 'God's Blueprint For Bible Prophecy' also by Kay Arthur on the book of Daniel

I began drafting this autobiography in Kenya in the eighties but had to lay it aside for several years while we lived in Israel, as well as the caring-years. I always knew there would be time to complete it once John was no longer with us.

When I first tried to write, I found the memories too painful to record or face, but six months later I have found it somewhat easier, as well as therapeutic. It is also important to write while memories are relatively fresh, but diary-keeping has paid off, and my hope is that this autobiography will be helpful to carer-readers and others from all walks of life.

272

I am submitting the manuscript to The Alzheimer's Society for their approval and expect to donate some of the royalties to them in gratitude for all their help and wise counsel during John's illness. I have found their Information Sheets on many topics invaluable.

The Prayer For Clevedon (P4C) intercession, meetings and breakfasts remain a focal-point month-by-month, as does Intercessors For Britain intercession with small, monthly meetings.

However, the number one priority will always be Israel and the Jewish people, who are the subject of my daily prayers and keeping up-to-date with events in Israel and The Diaspora. I pray that one day Clevedon will have its own prayer for Israel meeting. There are Israel-intercessors in nearby towns, but public transport limitations prevent me joining with them.

I observe the Lord's Feasts quietly alone at home, Erev Shabbat on Fridays and Shabbat on Saturdays - when I study the Torah and Haftarah set-portions, using these as a basis for prayer. Occasional coach day-trips still feature, mostly with a local Christian friend, and I have started attending UK-based conferences connected with Israel.

It is important to keep active and in contact as much as possible. Walking is my preferred method of exercise, but I do not enjoy doing so alone. The anaesthetic for my recent renal surgery has left me somewhat short of breath when walking uphill, but I trust that will normalise in time.

Today's sound of caring is expressed face-to-face, by phone or e-mail and supported in private-prayer for my global-family rather than in a reclusive, isolated 24/7 setting. I thank my heavenly Father for all I have learnt from my caring-experience, its loneliness and depression. I ask Him to use those vital lessons in brokenness and willingness to go the extra mile now in serving and offering care to His ancient people and others, in accordance with His plans and purposes for my future. *Nothing in His economy is ever wasted.* Praise Him!

Precept MinistriesUK,
P O Box 2129,
Salisbury,
SP2 2DL,
UK.

Tel: 01722 770028
Email: admin@precept.org.uk
Web: www.precept.org.uk

Donations from royalties from the sale of this book will be passed on to The Alzheimer's Society.